D1452892

Mary Day By Day

Mary Day By Day

MARIAN MEDITATIONS FOR EVERY DAY TAKEN FROM THE HOLY BIBLE AND THE WRITINGS OF THE SAINTS

Introduction by

Rev. Charles G. Fehrenbach, C.SS.R.

Illustrated

CATHOLIC BOOK PUBLISHING CO.
New York

CONTENTS

NIHIL OBSTAT: Daniel V. Flynn, J.C.D..
Censor Librorum

IMPRIMATUR: ✛ Patrick J. Sheridan, D.D.
Vicar General, Archdiocese of New York

(T-180)

INTRODUCTION

"It is the nature of Jesus Christ to lead us surely to the Father. In the same way, it is the nature of the Blessed Virgin Mary to lead us surely to Jesus" (St. Louis Grignion de Montfort).

THERE is no end to Marian books—nor should there be. Some are for devotion, some for edification, some for enlightenment and instruction. What is eminently desirable is an all-purpose volume that incorporates all these desiderata in one small convenient frame.

In *Mary Day By Day* we have such a volume. The fusion of Scripture, reflection, and prayer in a delightfully brief potpourri more than adequately fills the need for a handy book of Marian devotion. The work is not haphazard but carefully selective. The reflections blend in with the Scripture quotes, and the prayers are redolent of both.

Mary Day By Day is definitely not a book to be read from beginning to end, not a thriller or a mystery to be taken on a plane or bus and read at one sitting. We know the ending even before we pick up the book. What we want to do here is savor its contents—in tiny, delectable portions.

The daily selection takes only a minute or two to read. That's why it serves the purpose of edifying the busy individual who has time only for a taste of inspiration, perhaps at the beginning of the day, or intermittently. For such a one the daily capsule will be meaningful and adequate. The volume serves as an ideal bedside book, one you can pick up at the end of a busy day as you reach for holy water and compose yourself for a peaceful sleep.

As implied, the book is not a gem to be treasured and hidden, but a *vademecum*, like the Rosary in your purse or pocket, to be utilized for solace or comfort in appropriate moments. The *Scripture* quotes stimulate to quick thought, the *Reflections* apply appropriately, and the *Prayers* synthesize the inspiration in both.

In conferring the title of Doctor of the Church on St. Alphonsus, the Holy See said of his masterpiece, *The Glories of Mary*, "This book satisfies the needs and taste of the most diverse readers. . . . It is a veritable mine of ecclesiastical lore and Marian theology." The same can be said of *Mary Day By Day*. Borrowing from St. Alphonsus' foreword to his own book: "May this book help us love Jesus and Mary and become saints. We cannot hope or pray for anything better."

Rev. Charles G. Fehrenbach, C.SS.R.

WILL put enmities between you and the woman, and between your seed and hers. He shall crush your head.

JAN.
1

—Gen 3:15

REFLECTION. The Old Testament recounts the period of salvation history that slowly prepared for the coming of Christ into the world.

It brings into gradually sharper focus the figure of the Woman, Mother of the Redeemer, already foreshadowed in the promise of victory over the serpent. —*Vatican II: The Church, 55*

PRAYER. *O Mary, you were chosen by God to be the Mother of the Redeemer. Protect me always from evil and obtain eternal salvation for me in heaven with you and your Son Jesus.*

 ONCERNING mutual charity there is no need for us to write you, since you yourselves have learned from God to love each other.

JAN.
2

—1 Thes 4:9

REFLECTION. The most powerful means we have for drawing down the benevolence of Mary toward us is a virtue.

That virtue is love for our neighbor:

—*St. Gregory Nazianzen*

PRAYER. *O Mary, you are partial toward those who imitate your Divine Son in love for their neighbor. Teach me to love my neighbor in the many circumstances of life, no matter what the cost.*

SHE is the breath of the might of God and a pure emanation of the glory of the Almighty; therefore, nought that is defiled can enter into her. —Wis 7:25

JAN.
3

REFLECTION. The Eternal Father delights in regarding the Heart of the Blessed Virgin Mary as the masterpiece of His hands.

The Son delights in it as the Heart of His Mother, the source from which He received the Blood that redeemed us. The Holy Spirit dwells in Mary as in His temple. —St. John Vianney

PRAYER. *O Mary, you are the beloved Daughter of God the Father, the exalted Mother of God the Son, and the pure Bride of God the Holy Spirit. Teach me to know and love the Most Blessed Trinity.*

ADAM was formed first, then Eve. And, Adam was not the one deceived; it was the woman who was deceived and was in sin. —1 Tim 2:13-14

JAN.
4

REFLECTION. Eve was the cause of death for human beings. Through her, death came into the world.

Mary, on the other hand, was the cause of life. Through her, Life was born unto us.

—St. Epiphanius

PRAYER. *O Mary, you are the true Eve, which means "Mother of all the living." You brought Jesus into the world and He obtained eternal life for all. Let me never lose it.*

EHOLD, the virgin will be with child and will bring forth a son, and they will call his name Emmanuel, which means "God with us."
—Mt 1:23

REFLECTION. The Virgin Mother gave birth from her fruitful womb and inviolate body to Him Who became visible for us, to Him by Whom she had been created.

While conceiving, she was a Virgin; while giving birth, she was a virgin; a virgin in her pregnancy; a virgin while carrying her son; a virgin forever! —*St. Augustine*

PRAYER. *O Mary, grant me the grace to prize the virtue of purity highly and practice it sedulously. Help me always to put my trust in you and find refuge in your motherly intercession.*

———

ND entering the house [the Magi] found the child with Mary his mother. They bowed down and worshiped him. —Mt 2:11

REFLECTION. At the moment when Mary presents her Son to the Magi, she not only performs a personal action as Mother but also acts as the figure of the Church.

As the mother of all peoples, the Church in the person of Mary initiates her work of evangelization. —*Pope John Paul II*

PRAYER. *O Mary, you initiated the work of evangelization by presenting Jesus to the Magi. Help me to radiate Jesus to others every day of my life by all that I say and do.*

THE mother of Jesus said . . . , "There is no more wine." And Jesus said, . . . "My hour has not yet come." His Mother said to the attendants, "Do whatever he tells you." —Jn 2:3-5

REFLECTION. Let Mary never be far from your lips or heart. And to obtain the fruit of her prayers, do not forget the example of her life.

With her support, you will never fall. Beneath her protection, you will never fear. Under her guidance, you will never tire. And with her help, you will reach your heavenly goal.

—*St. Bernard*

PRAYER. *O Mary, enable me to heed your words as the servers did. Let me always do whatever Jesus tells me, so that He may effect in me the miracle of eternal bliss in heaven.*

GOD sent his Son born of a woman, born under the law, to redeem those under the law, so that we might receive the full rights of adoption. —Gal 4:4-5

REFLECTION. God has decreed that the whole' of the Redemption should be accomplished through Mary, with Mary, and in Mary.

Just as nothing was created without Christ, so nothing has been re-created without the Blessed Virgin. —*St. Peter Damian*

PRAYER. *O Mary, through you the world has been re-created by Jesus. Help me to contribute to this re-creation by performing all activities in union with you and your Divine Son.*

DAM called his wife Eve, because she would become the mother of all the living.

—Gen 3:20

REFLECTION. We are all children of Eve according to the flesh and children of the Blessed Virgin according to the spirit. For all of us, Mary has the love of a mother and the courage of a defender.

All find room in her. Sinners find pardon through her prayers, and the righteous are preserved in grace. —*St. John of Avila*

PRAYER. *O Mary, you are always a mother to me. Let me be always your child. Help me to come to you in all my joys as well as sorrows.*

Y sister, my spouse, is a garden enclosed, an enclosed garden, a fountain sealed up. —SS 4:12

REFLECTION. Happy are those to whom the Holy Spirit reveals the Secret of Mary in order that they may come to know her.

Happy are those to whom He opens the "Enclosed Garden" that they may enter and to whom He gives access to the "Sealed Fountain" that they may drink of the living waters of grace. —*St. Louis Grignion de Montfort*

PRAYER. *O Mary, help me to know you and be devoted to you more each day, so that I may obtain the graces God wants to bestow on me.*

EEP my commands and you shall live; **JAN.**
guard my teaching as the apple of
your eye. Bind them on your fingers; **11**
write them on the tablet of your heart.
—Prov 7:2-3

REFLECTION.   Entrust your cause to her who is
the Mother of Mercy, and zealously offer her
day by day most special marks of reverence.

Endeavor to maintain within both body and
soul the spotlessness of her purity, and walk in
her footsteps, humbly and gently like her.

—*St. Bonaventure*

PRAYER.   *O Mary, let me be devoted to you in
heart and soul ever more and more. And help
me to put that devotion into practice daily by
more closely imitating your life and virtues.*

Y me kings reign, and lawmakers de- **JAN.**
cree justice. By me princes govern, and
the mighty establish justice. **12**
—Prov 8:15-16

REFLECTION.   To serve Mary and to be her
courtier is the greatest honor we can possibly
possess.

For to serve the Queen of Heaven is already
to reign on high, and to live under her commands is a greater thing than to govern!

—*St. John Damascene*

PRAYER.   *O Mary, you are the Queen of
Heaven and Earth. Grant me the privilege of
serving you with love and fidelity all my life.
Let me realize that in serving you I am serving
Christ the Lord.*

FOR whoever finds me finds life and receives salvation from the Lord. But whoever does not find me hurts himself. They love death who hate me. —Prov 8:35-36

JAN.
13

REFLECTION. In the order of grace, God usually communicates Himself to human beings only through Mary.

If we want to go to Him and be united with Him, we must use the very means he used to come down to us. That means is a true devotion to our Lady. —*St. Louis Grignion de Montfort*

PRAYER. *O Mary, you are our most powerful intermediary with Christ and thus with the Blessed Trinity. Teach me what God desires of me, and help me to go to Jesus through you.*

YOU shall separate three cities. . . [where] a person who kills another may take refuge . . . to save his life when [he] unintentionally kills his neighbor. —Deut 19:2-4

JAN.
14

REFLECTION. Seek refuge in Mary because she is the city of refuge. We know that Moses set up three cities of refuge for anyone who inadvertently killed his neighbor.

Now the Lord has established a refuge of mercy, Mary, even for those who deliberately commit evil. Mary provides shelter and strength for the sinner. —*St. Anthony of Padua*

PRAYER. *O Mary, if I am ever so unfortunate as to lose God's grace, move me to take refuge in you. Help me to flee to my city of refuge, for you will lead me to Jesus.*

O you, O men, I call; my appeal is to all mankind. You simple ones, gain prudence; you fools, gain understanding.
—Prov 8:4-5

JAN.
15

REFLECTION. Those who want to prevent their heart from being pervaded by the evils of earth should entrust it to the Blessed Virgin, our Lady and our Mother.

They will then regain it in heaven, freed from all evils. —*St. Francis de Sales*

PRAYER. *O Mary, move me to entrust my heart and affections to you. By your prayers keep me from all evil and firmly attached to your Divine Son forever.*

ORRIBLE is the death [an evil tongue] inflicts; the netherworld is preferable to it. It has no power over the just; they will not be burned in its flames.
—Sir 28:21-22

JAN.
16

REFLECTION. Mary's words were discreet, and her voice was measured.

She did not shout and she was careful not to say anything bad about another person—nor even to listen willingly to wrong that was spoken. —*St. Athanasius*

PRAYER. *O Mary, you are the Model of Right Speech. Help me to avoid idle gossip as well as intemperate words. Let me make use of right speech to communicate with and help others rather than confuse and hurt them.*

HE angel Gabriel was sent from God . . . to a virgin . . . a descendant of David, and the virgin's name was Mary. And when the angel had come to her, he said, "Hail, full of grace! The Lord is with you." —Lk 1:26-28

JAN. 17

REFLECTION. The salvation of the whole world began with the "Hail Mary."

Hence, the salvation of each person is also attached to this prayer.

—*St. Louis Grignion de Montfort*

PRAYER. *O Mary, let the great prayer to you be on my lips morning, noon, and night. Enable me to say it especially at the hour of my death—for you will ensure my salvation.*

───────────

 . . . dwell in counsel and in learned thoughts. . . . Counsel and sound judgment are mine; mine are prudence and power. —Prov 8:12-14

JAN. 18

REFLECTION. When we dedicate ourselves to Mary, we become instruments in her hands just as she is an instrument in God's hands.

Let us then be guided by her, for she will provide for the needs of body and soul and overcome all difficulties and anxieties.

—*St. Maximilian Kolbe*

PRAYER. *O Mary, in all my trials and difficulties let me have recourse to Jesus through your intercession. And when I call upon you, please comfort me and lead me to your Divine Son.*

ITH me are riches and glory, endur-
ing riches and justice. My fruit is
better than pure gold, and my blossoms than rare silver. —Prov 8:18-19

JAN.
19

REFLECTION.   Mary is the stem of the beautiful flower on which the Holy Spirit rests with the fullness of His gifts. Hence, those who want to obtain the seven gifts of the Spirit must seek the flower of the Holy Spirit on the stem [Mary].

We go to Jesus through Mary, and through Jesus we find the grace of the Holy Spirit.

—St. Bonaventure

PRAYER.   *O Mary, You are the Spouse of the Holy Spirit. Through Jesus, help me to reach the Spirit and obtain His surpassing gifts, so that I may live forever in the grip of the Spirit.*

E who is mighty has done great things
for me, and holy is his name. His mercy
is from generation to generation on
those who fear him.   —Lk 1:49-50

JAN.
20

REFLECTION.   While remaining the Mother of our Judge, Mary is a mother to us, full of mercy.

She constitutes our protection. She keeps us close to Christ, and she faithfully takes the matter of our salvation into her charge.

—St. Peter Canisius

PRAYER.   *O Mary, God filled you with grace and made you a Co-Redeemer with Christ your Son. Let me have constant recourse to you and attain the salvation you helped win for all.*

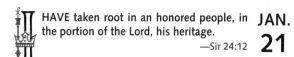 **I** HAVE taken root in an honored people, in the portion of the Lord, his heritage.

—Sir 24:12

JAN. 21

REFLECTION. Many will not let devotion to the Blessed Virgin even take root in their hearts. But blessed is the person who accepts this grace and keeps it.

Such a devotion dwells in all who are the Lord's heritage—in all who will praise Him eternally in heaven. *—St. Alphonsus Liguori*

PRAYER. *O Mary, let me foster devotion to you within my heart. May one day not go by without my turning to you in prayer and meditation.*

 H AVING therefore these promises, beloved, let us purify ourselves from every defilement of flesh and spirit, perfecting holiness in the fear of God.

—2 Cor 7:1

JAN. 22

REFLECTION. Those who have great devotion to Mary not only will be saved but also will, through her intercession, become great Saints.

Furthermore, their holiness will grow from day to day. *—St. Vincent Palotti*

PRAYER. *O Mary, grant me such deep devotion to you that it will lead me to thirst after holiness. Make me realize that my first purpose in life is to be holy with the aid of the grace Jesus won for me.*

THE light will be among you only a little longer. Walk while there still is light, before darkness overtakes you. Whoever walks in the dark knows not where he is going. —Jn 12:35

REFLECTION.   Go to Mary, then. Praise her, and you will be enlightened.

For it is through her that the true Light shines on the sea of this world. —*St. Ildephonsus*

PRAYER.   *O Mary, grant me always to have the Light of the World. Help me to walk in the Light of Christ all my days, so that I may know where I am going and avoid all evil.*

BLESSED is the man watching daily at my gates, waiting at my doorways.
—Prov 8:34

REFLECTION.   My most pleasant task is saying my Rosary and praying to my heavenly Mother.

It is the most pure joy of my heart!
—*St. Francis de Sales*

PRAYER.   *O Mary, my Mother in heaven, let me pray to you each day and say my Rosary. Help me to regard this as my heart's purest joy and my soul's greatest delight.*

EVERYONE who asks, receives; and the one who searches, finds; and to the one who knocks, it shall be opened.

—Lk 11:10

REFLECTION. In His eagerness to show you, mercy, God has given His Son as your Advocate.

And then to make your confidence even stronger, He has given you another Advocate, who obtains through her prayers whatever she asks. Go to Mary, and you will see salvation.

—*St. Alphonsus Liguori*

PRAYER. *O Mary, God has given you to me as a most powerful Advocate. Let me call upon you in any trouble and especially in time of danger to my eternal salvation.*

———————————

 SET me like a seal over your heart, like a seal on your arm; for love is strong as death, and jealousy as hard as the netherworld; its flames are a blazing fire.

—SS 8:6

REFLECTION. O Mother of love, you have given me your Heart.

Now take firm possession of my heart and offer it completely to the pure love and sole glory of your beloved Son. —*St. John Eudes*

PRAYER. *O Mary, you love all your spiritual children with a never-ending love. Grant me an undying love for you and your Divine Son Jesus both in time and for all eternity.*

COME, eat my bread, and drink the wine I have mixed for you! . . . For by me your days will be many and years will be added to your life.

JAN.
27

—Prov 9:5, 11

REFLECTION. You never think of Mary without Mary thinking of God on your behalf.

Neither do you ever praise and honor God without Mary praising and honoring God in union with you. —*St. Louis Grignion de Montfort*

PRAYER. *O Mary, I thank God for giving you to human beings as our intercessor. Help me to collaborate with you in praising God and in saving the souls of those whom Jesus came to redeem.*

I AM the root and the descendant of David as well as the bright morning star.

JAN.
28

—Rev 22:16

REFLECTION. The Blessed Virgin Mary is called the Star of the Sea.

Those who sail the ocean seas are guided to the port they seek by carefully observing the stars. In the same way, Christians are guided to heavenly glory by keeping their eyes on Mary. —*St. Thomas Aquinas*

PRAYER. *O Mary, bright Morning Star for all the earth, let the rays of your Son's grace shine ever upon me. Be my loving guide until at last I arrive safely at the heavenly shore.*

OU have wounded my heart. . . . You have wounded my heart with one glance of your eyes, with one link of your necklace. **JAN. 29**

—SS 4:9

REFLECTION. In danger, anguish, or doubt, think of Mary and call upon her!

Following her, you will never lose your way. Praying to her, you will never sink into despair. Contemplating her, you will never go wrong.

—*St. Bernard*

PRAYER. *O Mary, let my mind and heart be ever focused on you. Watch over me as you lovingly watched over Jesus in His childhood during the Hidden Years at Nazareth.*

 LOVE those who love me, and those who watch for me find me. **JAN. 30**

—Prov 8:17

REFLECTION. Blessed are those who abandon themselves into our Lady's hands.

Their names are written in the Book of Life.

—*St. Bonaventure*

PRAYER. *O Mary, I entrust myself into your hands. I give you my body and my soul, my thoughts and my actions, my life and my death. Help me to love Jesus above all things.*

Y son, forget not my teaching, and let your heart keep my commands; for they will bring you length of days and years of peace. —Prov 3:1-2

JAN. 31

REFLECTION. When Mary became the Mother of Jesus, true God and true Man, she also became our Mother.

In His great mercy, Jesus wished to call us His brothers and sisters, and by this name He constituted us adopted children of Mary.

—*St. John Bosco*

PRAYER. *O Mary, let me be devoted to you as my Mother and to Jesus as my Brother. Help me to follow your teaching, which is that of your Divine Son.*

 ALL you who pass by the way, look and see whether there is any sorrow like my sorrow. —Lam 1:12

FEB. 1

REFLECTION. Human beings will never comprehend sufficiently the anguish and immensity of Mary's sorrows.

Very few Christians partake of those sufferings and even fewer offer any consolation to her. —*St. Bridget*

PRAYER. *O Mary, let me dwell constantly on your part in the Redemption, which entailed great sorrow for you. Teach me to compassionate with you in your sufferings and unite myself to them.*

AND suddenly the Lord whom you seek, and the Messenger of his covenant whom you desire, shall come to his temple, says the Lord of hosts.

FEB. 2

—Mal 3:1

REFLECTION. The Presentation in the Temple . . . is the celebration of the Mystery of Salvation accomplished by Christ.

The Blessed Virgin was intimately associated in this Mystery as the Mother of the Suffering Servant of Yahweh, as the one who performs a mission belonging to ancient Israel, and as the model of the new People of God. —*Pope Paul VI*

PRAYER. *O Mary, you felt joy and sorrow during the Presentation. Teach me to accept both joy and sorrow with equanimity, since God works everything out for our good.*

FOR who is God but the Lord? What rock is there except our God? God who has girt me with strength and kept my way secure.

FEB. 3

—Ps 18:32-33

REFLECTION. We must look upon Mary as an accomplished model of every virtue and perfection that the Holy Spirit has fashioned in any simple creature.

We will then be able to imitate her in the way suitable to each of us.

—*St. Louis Grignion de Montfort*

PRAYER. *O Mary, you are the Model of every virtue. Help me to study your life and imitate your virtues in the way God intends for me.*

BRAM believed God and it was credited to him as an act of righteousness. **FEB. 4**
—Gen 15:6

REFLECTION. Mary is the heir and fulfillment of the faith of Abraham. Just as he is regarded as "our father," so Mary must with greater reason be regarded as "our Mother" in faith.

Through Mary's faith and obedience, all the families of the earth are blessed, in accord with the promise made to Abraham (see Gen 12:3).

—*Pope John Paul II*

PRAYER. *O Mary, you are my Mother in faith. Let me model my faith after your own. Increase it from day to day, so that upon my death that faith may be changed into vision in heaven.*

 ARY said, "Behold, the handmaid of the Lord. May it be done to me according to your word." **FEB. 5**
—Lk 1:38

REFLECTION. See the humility. Note the devotion. She who has been chosen to be the Mother of the Lord calls herself His handmaid!

In no way does she become haughty over this promise of such an exalted position. She does not take as a right what is freely given as a grace. —*St. Ambrose*

PRAYER. *O Mary, you remained humble despite the great grace bestowed on you as Mother of God. Help me to remain humble in all situations for it is God Who does all the good in us*

24

OW therefore, children, listen to me. Hear instruction and be wise and do not reject it.

FEB.

6

—Prov 8:32-33

REFLECTION. No one, O most holy Mary, can know God but through you. No one can be saved or redeemed but through you, O Mother of God.

No one obtains mercy but through you, O full of grace. —*St. Germanus*

PRAYER. *O Mary, reveal Jesus to me more and more. In getting to know the Son, may I also get to know the Father—for Jesus said that this is eternal life.*

 E sober and alert. Your enemy the devil goes about like a roaring lion seeking someone to devour. Resist him, and stand firm in the faith.

FEB.

7

—1 Pet 5:8-9

REFLECTION. The devil is always looking for someone to devour.

In the same way, Mary is always looking for someone she can help in any way.

—*St. Leo the Great*

PRAYER. *O Mary, you are especially vigilant in protecting those devoted to you. Defend me from the snares of the devil and keep me ever safe in your loving care.*

EFORE they cry out, I will answer; while they are yet speaking, I will hear.
—Isa 65:24

REFLECTION. Mary is more prompt than all the Saints in coming to our aid. She has a great desire to comfort us.

The moment she is invoked, she welcomes our prayers and grants us her assistance.
—*St. Alphonsus Liguori*

PRAYER. *O Mary, you are ready to hear us at every moment. Let me remain united with you all my days and seek your powerful help in time of trial and temptation.*

 HE Lord possessed me in the beginning of his ways, before anything was made. From eternity I was brought forth, before the earth was made.
—Prov 8:22-23

REFLECTION. The Holy Spirit spoke of Mary by the mouth of the Prophets, foretold her by His oracles, and drew her portrait by means of figures.

He promised her in the events that preceded her and completed her in the events that followed her.
—*St. Ildephonsus*

PRAYER. *O Mary, both before and after your birth you were looked after by God's wonderful Providence. Make me realize that the same Providence is also guiding every event in this world and in my life.*

GREAT sign appeared in heaven, a woman robed with the sun, with the moon beneath her feet, and a crown of twelve stars upon her head.

FEB.
10

—Rev 12:1

REFLECTION.   Mary is the glory of Virgins, the joy of Mothers, the bulwark of the Faithful, and the crown of the Church.

She is the model of the true Faith, the seat of Piety, the robe of Virtue, and the dwelling-place of the Holy Trinity.   —*St. Proclus*

PRAYER.   *O Mary, you desire to bring forth true believers in your Divine Son. Help me to be a lifelong follower of Jesus and so deserve to enjoy eternal bliss with you in heaven.*

 HAVE sanctified this temple that you have built to put my name upon it forever, and my eyes and my heart will always be there.   —1 Ki 9:3

FEB.
11

REFLECTION.   In no other spot as much as Lourdes do we feel so impelled toward prayer, forgetfulness of self, and charity. The most fervent are attracted to a life more totally offered to God's service.

The less fervent become aware of their tepidity and rediscover the way of prayer. Hardened sinners and unbelievers are often touched by grace.   —*Pope Pius XII*

PRAYER.   *O Mary, turn my heart into a miniature Lourdes where I can honor you each day and receive spiritual strength for my earthly journey.*

SPREAD out my branches like a terebinth, and my branches are glorious and so graceful. Like the vine I bud forth delights, and my blossoms become fair and abundant fruit. —Sir 24:16-17

FEB. 12

REFLECTION. The grace of Mary is outstanding indeed, superabundant and overflowing.

It gave glory to heaven, begot God on earth, filled the Angels with joy, and brought peace to the world.

—*St. Lawrence Justinian*

PRAYER. *O Mary, in you is all grace and you hold the key to the grace of Christ. Obtain for me all the graces I need in my state in life and help me to cooperate with them faithfully.*

 HEN in a dream he saw a ladder resting on the ground, with its top reaching to heaven; and God's angels were ascending and descending. —Gen 28:12

FEB. 13

REFLECTION. Mary may be truly called the Stairway of Heaven.

By her God descended from heaven to the world so that by her we might ascend from earth to heaven. —*St. Fulgentius*

PRAYER. *O Mary, you are our Stairway to Paradise. Teach me to live in such a way that I may climb a step closer to heaven with each passing day and ultimately attain the Beatific Vision forever.*

ET all who fly to you for refuge rejoice and exult forever. Watch over them, that those who love your name may rejoice in you.
—Ps 5:12

FEB.
14

REFLECTION.   Place your trust in Mary and go to her in your sorrows.

She will strengthen your will, heal the wounds of your soul, and give you new courage.
—*Venerable Francis Libermann*

PRAYER.   *O Mary, I place all my trust in you. Stay with me always, despite my weaknesses and all kinds of difficulties. Renew my flagging courage and never forsake me.*

HEN you pray, go to your room, shut the door, and pray to your Father in secret. Then your Father who sees what is done in secret will repay you.
—Mt 6:6

FEB.
15

REFLECTION.   Mary's whole life was one continual colloquy.

It was a colloquy with the heavenly Father and with the Holy Spirit, her Divine Spouse.
—*St. Francis de Sales*

PRAYER.   *O Mary, you are our exemplar of prayer. Teach me the science of praying. Help me to set aside each day time for prayer—with the Father, the Holy Spirit, and your Divine Son Jesus.*

TOGETHER with her, all good things came to me, and in her hands are countless riches. And I delighted in them all, since . . . she was their mother. —Wis 7:11-12

REFLECTION. Mary is the Mother and Dispensatrix of all grace.

Every servant of this great Queen should affirm: "Thanks to my devotion to Mary, all blessings have come to me." —*St. Antoninus*

PRAYER. *O Mary, all that is good in me comes from God through you. I offer you my humble gratitude and ask you to thank your Divine Son on my behalf.*

SAY to the daughter of Zion: See, your savior comes! Behold, his reward is with him, his recompense before him. —Isa 62:11

REFLECTION. Mary stands out among the poor and humble of the Lord, who confidently hope for and receive salvation from Him.

She is also the exalted Daughter of Zion in whom the times are fulfilled and the New Plan of salvation is established.

—*Vatican II:: The Church, 55*

PRAYER. *O Mary, you are the humble yet exalted Daughter of the Lord. Teach me true humility, which is so prized by your Divine Son.*

COUNT life of no importance to me, if only I may finish my course and the ministry given to me . . . to bear witness to the Gospel of the grace of God. –Act 20:24

FEB.
18

REFLECTION. O my Mother, let it be done to me! Let life be done to me! Let suffering be done to me!

Let even death be done to me, O Mother, as long as I remain united with your Immaculate Heart!
—*St. Bernadette*

PRAYER. *O Mary, I offer myself entirely to God through your hands and after your example. I accept whatever He wills for me and ask you to keep me faithful to this resolve.*

———————

 VEN though I should walk in the valley of death I will fear no evil, for you are with me. Your rod and your staff comfort me. —Ps 23:4

FEB.
19

REFLECTION. Mary, Mother of the Good Shepherd and our Mother, is renowned for obtaining all kinds of good things for her children.

May she always be our trust and our hope!
—*St. Germanus*

PRAYER. *O Mary, you continually watch over the flock of your Divine Son. Be ever at my side with your unfailing aid, so that I may follow the Good Shepherd closely and dwell in the house of the Lord forever.*

BLESSED are you who have believed because the things promised you by the Lord shall be fulfilled.

FEB.
20

—Lk 1:45

REFLECTION.   Mary was blessed by conceiving the flesh of Christ.

But she was even more blessed by receiving the faith of Christ!   —*St. Augustine*

PRAYER.   *O Mary, you are forever identified as "the Virgin who believed." Grant me some measure of the faith you exhibited. Help me to believe in God's Word more and more every day.*

———————

DO not be deceived. . . . Every good and perfect gift is from above, coming down from the Father of lights, with whom there is no change, nor shadow of alteration.   —Jas 1:16-17

FEB.
21

REFLECTION.   Devotion to the Blessed Virgin in no way detracts from the glory of God.

Rather it leads us directly back to that Author of all good Who has willed her to be so great and so pure.   —*Pope Pius XII*

PRAYER.   *O Mary, honor paid to you always leads to the praise of God. Grant me a true devotion to you, so that I may be more deeply devoted to your Divine Son, Jesus, Who is our Redeemer.*

YOU are Peter, and upon this rock I will build my Church, and the gates of hell shall not overcome it. —Mt 16:18

FEB. 22

REFLECTION. Peter was entrusted with the Church, the Mother of human beings, but John was entrusted with Mary, the Mother of God.

John loved her like his own mother and was loved by her as her own son. —*St. Peter Damien*

PRAYER. *O Mary, you are the Mother of the Church as well as the Mother of God. Keep me close to you so that I may be a true child of God and a faithful member of His holy Church.*

 WHO singles you out? What do you have that you have not received? And if you have received it, why do you boast as if you did not receive it? —1 Cor 4:7

FEB. 23

REFLECTION. How dear are humble souls to Mary! She recognizes and loves those who love her and is near to all who call upon her.

This is especially true of those who she sees are like her in chastity and humility.

—*St. Bernard*

PRAYER. *O Mary, you love humility because you know how little we are when set against God's greatness. Help me to be ever grateful to the Lord for His overwhelming goodness to me.*

DO not remain in the company of drunkards nor with those who gorge themselves at meals. For they soon come to ruin and are clothed in rags. —Prov 23:20-21

FEB. 24

REFLECTION. Mary would never have found such grace had she not been moderate in her food.

For grace and gluttony cannot exist together. —*St. Bonaventure*

PRAYER. *O Mary, you were a model of self-control with your food. Help me to avoid any kind of gluttony so that I may always be ready to cooperate with the grace of Jesus in me.*

———————

THE angel answered and said to [Mary], "The Holy Spirit will come upon you, and the power of the Most High will overshadow you." —Lk 1:35

FEB. 25

REFLECTION. The Holy Spirit heated, inflamed, and melted Mary with love, as fire does to iron.

Thus, the flame of this Holy Spirit was seen, and nothing was felt but the fire of the love of God. —*St. Ildephonsus*

PRAYER. *O Mary, you were filled with the power of the Holy Spirit and with overwhelming love for God. Obtain for me a greater love for God that will overflow in more frequent prayer and a more dedicated Christian life.*

REMEMBER us, O Lord. Reveal yourself in this time of our tribulation, and give me courage, O King of gods and Master of every dominion. Est C: 23 (14:12)

FEB. 26

REFLECTION. Great was the mercy of Mary toward the afflicted when she was still on earth.

But it is far greater now that she is in heaven. For she better sees the miseries suffered by human beings. —*St. Bonaventure*

PRAYER. *O Mary, you continually come to the aid of the afflicted in this world. Pray for me during my earthly exile and bring me safely to heaven's blissful shore.*

GIVE and it shall be given to you; a good measure . . . shall they pour into your lap. For with the same measure that you use, it shall be measured out for you. —Lk 6:38

FEB. 27

REFLECTION. Blessed are they, says the Divine Mother, who pay attention to my charity and, in imitation of me, practice it toward others.

Our charity toward our neighbor will be the measure of that which God and Mary will show us. —*St. Alphonsus Liguori*

PRAYER. *O Mary, you always showed true charity toward others. Enable me to overcome my human prejudices and be charitable to all people, for they are my brothers and sisters in Christ.*

T is good for me to be close to God, to trust always in the Lord God. I will proclaim all your deeds.

FEB. 28

—Ps 73:28

REFLECTION. Hope takes its rise in faith. God enlightens us by faith to know His goodness and the promises He has made and so rise by hope to the desire of possessing Him.

Since Mary had the virtue of faith in the highest degree, she also had hope to that same degree. —*St. Alphonsus Liguori*

PRAYER. *O Mary, you are the Mother of Hope. Help me never to despair. In every difficulty, lead me to rely on God's promises and place my hope in Him completely.*

 N a robe of striking colors she is led to the king; behind her the virgin companions are brought to you. They are borne in with gladness and rejoicing; they enter the palace of the king.

MAR. 1

—Ps 45:15-16

REFLECTION. With reason is Mary called "the Virgin of virgins"; for she, without the counsel or example of others, was the first who offered her virginity to God.

Thus did she bring all virgins who imitate her to God, as David foretold (in Psalm 45).

—*St. Albert the Great*

PRAYER. *O Mary, you are the Virgin of virgins. Let me be true to my state in life. May I prize purity as the best means of remaining united with God.*

THE Lord our God is one! You shall love the Lord your God with your whole heart, with your whole soul, with your whole mind, and with all your strength. —Mk 12:29-30

MAR.
2

REFLECTION. Divine love so inflamed Mary that nothing earthly could enter her affections.

She was always enkindled with God's heavenly ardor and, so to speak, inebriated with it.
—*St. Sophronius*

PRAYER. *O Mary, the eyes of your soul were constantly on God with love. Help me to love God with an undivided heart and with the full force of all my being.*

IWAS with him forming all things and was delighted every day playing in his presence, playing in the world. —Prov 8:30

MAR.
3

REFLECTION. So pleasing to God was Mary's humility that He was constrained by His goodness to entrust to her the Word, His only Son.

And it was that dearest Mother who gave Him to us. —*St. Catherine of Siena*

PRAYER. *O Mary, Mother of humility, teach me the humility that draws your Divine Son to the soul. May I desire to offer whatever I have to Jesus and do everything for His glory.*

HOLOCAUSTS and sin offerings did not please you. Then I said, "As is written of me in the head of the book, Behold, I come to do your will, O God." —Heb 10:6-7

MAR. 4

REFLECTION. Mary's sole object in this world was to keep her eyes constantly focused on God so as to discover His will.

Then when she had found out what God wanted, she did it. —*St. Bernardine of Siena*

PRAYER. *O Mary, you are the obedient Daughter of the Father who cooperated with Him in the salvation worked by Jesus. In every situation make known God's will to me and help me to carry it out willingly.*

GOD is love, and whoever abides in love lives in God and God in him. In this way, love is brought to perfection among us. —1 Jn 4:16

MAR. 5

REFLECTION. The Heart of Mary constituted a perfect empire for the Divine Love, which always reigned therein.

And it caused to reign therein all the laws of God, all the maxims of heaven, and all the Christian virtues. —*St. John Eudes*

PRAYER. *O Mary, your Heart was a burning vessel of God's love. Fill my heart with love for God and let me thank Him every day for His great love in sending His only Son to obtain my salvation.*

RECEIVE my instruction and not silver, and choose knowledge before gold. For wisdom is better than precious stones, and no object of desire can compare with her. —Prov 8:10-11 **MAR. 6**

REFLECTION. Read attentively the book of purity that is Mary, written by the finger of God.

Read the holiness, the love, the kindness, the humility—in short, read the vast fullness of all the virtues. —*St. Thomas of Villanova*

PRAYER. *O Mary, help me to learn from you how to lead a Christian life. Let me strive to imitate the virtues you exhibited, for you were the closest follower of your Divine Son Jesus on earth.*

———————

 JESUS told [the disciples] a parable about praying without losing heart. —Lk 18:1 **MAR. 7**

REFLECTION. After Jesus Christ, the Divine Mother was the most perfect in prayer of all who have ever been or will ever be.

Mary's prayer was continual and persevering! —*St. Albert the Great*

PRAYER. *O Mary, you are the Model of Prayer. Teach me to love and appreciate prayer as you did. Help me to pray morning, noon, or night, in every circumstance of life and in any personal mood.*

HOEVER is greatest among you shall be your servant. Whoever exalts himself shall be humbled; and whoever humbles himself shall be exalted. —Mt 23:11-12

REFLECTION. Apart from the Son of God, no creature in the world was so exalted as Mary.

For no creature in the world ever humbled itself so much as she did!

—St. Bernardine of Siena

PRAYER. *O Mary, you are exalted over all because you were the humblest of all. Let me imitate your humility and merit one day to share in your exaltation in heaven.*

PATH shall be there called the holy way; the unclean shall not pass over it. . . . And on it shall walk the delivered. —Isa 35:8-9

REFLECTION. May the Blessed Virgin Mary help me to live a holy life and die a holy death.

Then at the last instants of my life, may she come to my assistance and lead me to heaven.

—St. Dominic Savio

PRAYER. *O Mary, you led St. Dominic along the "holy way" during his short life on earth. Lead me too along this way of holiness so that I may one day join him and you in the eternal holiness of heaven.*

UN to win. Everyone who competes for a prize abstains in every way. . . . I chastise my body and train it lest after having preached to others, I myself shall become a castaway. —1 Cor 9:24-27

MAR. 10

REFLECTION. Those who love Mary must silence within themselves the desires of the senses.

They must also silence the disordered longings of the passions. —*St. John Eudes*

PRAYER. *O Mary, you well know all the temptations that exist in the world. Help me to curb my evil desires and practice self-discipline, so that I may safeguard my union with your Divine Son.*

 RAY without ceasing. In all circumstances give thanks, for this is God's will for you in Christ Jesus.
—1 Thes 5:17-18

MAR. 11

REFLECTION. During her earthly life Mary lived in continual prayer.

Therefore, all who are devoted to her must pray—and pray continually.

—*St. Louis Grignion de Montfort*

PRAYER. *O Mary, you know the secret of prayer. Let me be convinced that more things are wrought by prayer than this world dreams of. Whenever I slack off in my prayer life, gently lead me back to it.*

AND whatever you do, in word or in acts, do it all in the name of the Lord Jesus, giving thanks to God the Father through him. —Col 3:17

MAR.
12

REFLECTION. We must accomplish all our actions through Mary, with Mary, and in Mary.

In that way, we will also accomplish them all through Jesus, with Jesus, and in Jesus.

—*St. Louis Grignion de Montfort*

PRAYER. *O Mary, through your Immaculate Heart I offer all my prayers, works, and sufferings to Jesus. I offer them for the intentions of His Sacred Heart and the salvation of the world.*

WHO shall ascend the mountain of the Lord? or who shall stand in his holy place? The one with innocent hands and a pure heart. —Ps 24:3-4

MAR.
13

REFLECTION. To whom shall we look except to you, O Mary?

Your most pure glance is on this poor world, enveloping and bathing it in an atmosphere of purity. —*Pope Pius XII*

PRAYER. *O Mary, you are the Immaculate Conception, "our tainted nature's solitary boast." Help me to have clean hands and a pure heart so that I can ascend to the heavenly mountain of the Lord.*

TEACH me to do your will, since you are my God. Your Spirit is good; may it lead me on level ground.

MAR.
14

—Ps 143:10

REFLECTION. This faithful handmaid never, in either thought or word or deed, contradicted the Most High.

Entirely despoiled of her own will, Mary lived always and in all things obedient to the will of God. —*St. Thomas of Villanova*

PRAYER. *O Mary, you obeyed God in all things. Help me to obey the Divine will for me down to the least detail, no matter how difficult it may seem. For in doing God's will is my good.*

WHOM do I have in heaven but you? And when I am in your presence, the earth delights me not. . . . God is my heart's strength and my heritage for ever. —Ps 73:25-26

MAR.
15

REFLECTION. Divine love so penetrated and filled the soul of Mary that no part of her was left untouched.

She loved with her whole heart, with her whole soul, with her whole strength, and was full of grace. —*St. Bernard*

PRAYER. *Mary, you chose God as the one thing necessary. Teach me to set my heart on God and help me to carry out His saving plan for me on earth.*

CONSIDER all as loss . . . so as to know him and the power of his resurrection and the sharing of his sufferings, becoming like him in death, and hoping somehow to attain the resurrection from the dead. —Phil 3:8-11

MAR. 16

REFLECTION. The Blessed Virgin advanced in her pilgrimage of faith and loyally persevered in her union with her Son unto the Cross. . . .

There she united herself with a maternal heart to His sufferings. —*Vat. II: Church, 59*

PRAYER. *O Mary, you suffered with Jesus as you stood beneath the Cross and you offered your suffering with His. Help me to accept my daily crosses without complaint and offer them for the good of the world.*

 HOEVER hears you hears me. Whoever rejects you rejects me. And whoever rejects me rejects him who sent me. —Lk 10:16

MAR. 17

REFLECTION. Do not be afraid of loving the Blessed Virgin too much. You can never love her enough.

And Jesus will be very happy, because the Blessed Virgin is His Mother.

—*St. Theresa of Lisieux*

PRAYER. *O Mary, when Christians show love and honor to you they show love and honor to your Son. Let my love for you grow every day and redound to the glory of Jesus and to my salvation.*

WOMAN has sorrow when about to give birth . . . ; but when the child has been brought forth . . . , she no longer remembers the pain because of her joy that a child is born into the world.

MAR. 18

—Jn 16:21

REFLECTION. Mary paid the debt of gratitude that was due from womankind because of Eve.

Not of man, but immaculately of her own self, she conceived of the Holy Spirit by the power of God. —*St. Cyril of Jerusalem*

PRAYER. *O Mary, by your conception of Jesus you furthered the Divine Plan of Salvation and laid the basis for a theology of woman. Let me learn from you how sublime is the role of women in the world.*

 OSEPH . . . did as the angel . . . had commanded him and took Mary as his wife. He did not know her until she brought forth a son, and he called him Jesus.

MAR. 19

—Mt 1:24-25

REFLECTION. The Church is indebted to Mary because it is Mary who gave the Church her King, Jesus Christ.

After the Blessed Virgin, it is to St. Joseph that the Church owes the most gratitude and veneration. —*St. Bernardine of Siena*

PRAYER. *O Mary, you loved Joseph and depended on him as the head of the Holy Family at Nazareth. Help me to have a great devotion to him and to call upon him in times of doubt and fear.*

ER I loved and from my youth sought her out. . . . She manifests her noble birth by union of life with God, for the Lord of all has loved her. —Wis 8:2-3

REFLECTION. My hope for you is that with every passing day and every passing moment you will get closer to Mary Immaculate.

May you come to know her ever better and love her ever more. —*St. Maximilian Kolbe*

PRAYER. *O Mary, you are the Immaculate Mother of God. Let me come to know you better and love you more each day. And let me cooperate with all the graces you dispense to me at every moment.*

 OU will sing as on a night when a festival is celebrated, and have joy of heart, as when people go with flutes to the mountain of God. —Isa 30:29

REFLECTION. Rejoice and be glad, for you have the Blessed Virgin for your Mother.

Serve her with great joy, for she is very deserving of it. Have recourse to her in all difficulties, and you will always be helped.

—*St. Joachima Vedruna de Mas*

PRAYER. *O Mary, I thank God for giving you to us as our Mother and I rejoice in your saving help. May I stay close to you in good times and in bad, for you are keenly interested in all that concerns me.*

THEN he said to the disciple, "Behold your mother." And from that moment the disciple took her into his home.
—Jn 19:27

MAR. 22

REFLECTION. The Blessed Virgin directs to us all the acts that every mother lavishes on her children.

She loves us, watches over us, protects us, and intercedes for us. —*Pope John XXIII*

PRAYER. *O Mary, you love me and take care of me like a true Mother. Let me have constant recourse to you in all my problems and benefit from your maternal assistance.*

CHRIST . . . suffered for you, leaving you an example that you may follow in his steps. "He committed no sin, and no deceit was uttered by his mouth." —1 Pet 2:21-22

MAR. 23

REFLECTION. The Blessed Virgin never committed any actual sin—not even a venial one. Otherwise, she would not have been a Mother, worthy of Jesus.

The Son would have shared the ignominy of the Mother, for He would have had a sinner for His Mother. —*St. Thomas Aquinas*

PRAYER. *O Mary, through the grace of Jesus you remained forever free from all sin. Obtain forgiveness of my past sins from your Divine Son and help me to avoid sin in the future.*

THE father of a just man greatly rejoices. . . . Let your father and mother be joyful; let her who bore you rejoice.
—Prov 23:24-25

REFLECTION.   There is no doubt whatever that all the praises we address to the Mother are also addressed to the Son and vice versa.

We cannot do honor to the Son without at the same time giving glory to the Mother.

—*St. Bernard*

PRAYER.   *O Mary, you are forever connected with Jesus as His Mother and as His closest disciple. Let me never hesitate to honor you for in doing so I am honoring your Divine Son.*

MARY, you have found grace with God. Behold, you will conceive in your womb and bring forth a son, and you shall call his name Jesus.
—Lk 1:31

REFLECTION.   O Mary, when Jesus was conceived in you, He found you a Virgin. After being born of you, He left you a Virgin.

He gives you fertility, but He does not violate your integrity.   —*St. Augustine*

PRAYER.   *O Mary, you were a Virgin in conceiving, in bearing your Child, and in dying. Teach me that with God nothing is impossible, and let me face life confidently with the aid of His grace.*

IVE praise O daughter of Zion. . . . Rejoice and exult with all your heart, O daughter of Jerusalem.

MAR. 26

—Zep 3:14

REFLECTION. What is the language of the Angel sent to the most pure Virgin? "Hail, full of grace, the Lord is with you."

He is a messenger of joy, and it is with joy that he opens the conversation. —*St. Sophronius*

PRAYER. *O Mary, what joy must have been yours at the news that the Son of God would be within you! Let me rejoice too in the knowledge that I also am called to bear Jesus within me through grace.*

 N the beginning, God created heaven and earth. . . . God said, "Let there be ['Fiat'] light," and there was light. . . .

MAR. 27

—Gen 1:1-3

REFLECTION. Scarcely had Mary uttered her Fiat ["Let it be done"] when the Son of God became also the Son of Mary.

O *Fiat* to be venerated above every other *Fiat!* For with a *Fiat* God created light, heaven, and earth; but with Mary's *Fiat* God became man, like us! —*St. Thomas of Villanova*

PRAYER. *O Mary, you cooperated fully in God's plan of salvation. Let me realize that God has given each of us something unique to do. Help me to say each day "Let it be done" to whatever God wants of me.*

EALTH and honor are from you, and you rule over all. In your hand are power and might; to give honor and strength to all.

MAR. 28

—1 Chr 29:12

REFLECTION. To be the Mother of God is the greatest grace that can be conferred on a creature.

God could make a greater world and a greater heaven, but He cannot exalt a creature more than by making her His Mother.

—*St. Bonaventure*

PRAYER. *O Mary, you are God's masterpiece and the jewel of the human race. Let me render to you the honor you deserve and render to God thanks for the great grace bestowed on us in you.*

Y dearest children . . . in Christ Jesus, through the Gospel, I am your father. Therefore, imitate me as I imitate Christ.

MAR. 29

—1 Cor 4:14-16

REFLECTION. Jesus entrusted me to His Mother and charged me to love her.

O Mary, you are my heavenly Mother. You will act toward me like any Mother toward her children! —*St. Gemma Galgani*

PRAYER. *O Mary, you are my spiritual Mother and the Mother of my salvation. Let me glory in your care and be obedient to your loving promptings during each day.*

HAVE loved you with an everlasting love; therefore, my mercy is upon you. And I will build you up again.

MAR.
30

—Jer 31:3-4

REFLECTION. O Mother of Love, I am not surprised that the excess of your love for your poor children is so admirable.

Indeed, such love forever sends into ecstasy the inhabitants of heaven. —*St. John Eudes*

PRAYER. *O Mary, your love for us knows no bounds and is beyond human comprehension. Help me always to reciprocate that love and come to you with childlike confidence and gratitude.*

 HEN he established the heavens I was there, when he enclosed the depths within their bounds.

MAR.
31

—Prov 8:27

REFLECTION. O Mary you possess the authority of a Mother toward God.

Therefore, it is impossible for you not to be heard, for God always treats you like His true and immaculate Mother. —*St. Germanus*

PRAYER. *O Mary, you have the ear of God because you are the Mother of God. Place before Him the needs of the whole world and keep me close to you at every moment.*

YOU have turned my mourning into dancing; in place of sackcloth you robed me in joy, that my soul may praise you forever. —Ps 30:12-13

APR.

1

REFLECTION. Mary is the arsenal of graces, and she rushes to the aid of her children.

She sustains, strengthens, and renews them by means of the heavenly favors she heaps on them. —*St. Paulinus*

PRAYER. *O Mary, you are very generous with the graces entrusted to you. Grant that I may not take the graces I receive for granted but instead ever seek to cooperate with them.*

HER riches I do not conceal. For she is an inexhaustible treasure for all; those who acquire her achieve friendship with God, commended to him by the gifts that derive from her instruction. —Wis 7:13-14

APR.

2

REFLECTION. Mary adorns her clients with her merits, assists them with her power, enlightens them with her light, and kindles them with her love.

She imparts her virtues to them and becomes their security, their intercessor, and their all with Jesus. —*St. Louis Grignion de Montfort*

PRAYER. *O Mary, you are a treasure to your, clients. Keep my relationship with you strong and vital. Let me never weary of practicing my devotion to you and help me spread it to others.*

YOU shall also forget misery . . . and brightness like the noonday shall come to you at evening. And you shall have confidence and rest secure.

**APR.
3**

—Job 11:16-18

REFLECTION. On every occasion and in every way, Mary comes to the aid of our misery, calms our fears, and perks up our faith.

She sustains our hope, dispels our misgivings, and remedies our laxity. —*St. Bernard*

PRAYER. *O Mary, you are our consolation and our help. Come to my aid especially in time of trial when I am vulnerable. Make me remember all that Jesus did for me and keep me faithful to Him.*

———

AGAIN Jesus spoke to them, saying, "I am the light of the world. Whoever follows me will not walk in the dark, but will have the light of life."

**APR.
4**

—Jn 8:12

REFLECTION. The name "Mary" means light or star of the sea.

For it was Mary who brought forth the Eternal Light, Jesus Christ! —*St. Isidore*

PRAYER. *O Mary, you are our shining star pointing the way to your Divine Son. Amid the darkness and evil running rampant in today's world, let me always keep my eyes on Jesus!*

BSERVE the upright and consider the just, for posterity awaits the man of peace. —Ps 37:37

APR.
5

REFLECTION. The Blessed Virgin Mary comforts and refreshes those who are in their last agony.

Then she also receives their souls at death.

—*St. Vincent Ferrer*

PRAYER. *O Mary, you are the Mother of a Happy Death. Take care of me in my last moments of life. Defend me from the wiles of the devil and receive me into paradise.*

AM wearied with groaning; night after night I flood my bed with weeping. I water my couch with tears; sorrow dims my eyes. —Ps 6: 7-8

APR.
6

REFLECTION. The Blessed Virgin Mary never departed—not even slightly—from the precepts and examples of her Divine Son.

This was true both in the ecstatic joy she experienced and in the trials and cruel sufferings she endured, which have made her the Queen of Martyrs. —*Pope Pius XII*

PRAYER. *O Mary, you remained united with God in spite of heartbreak and sorrow. Help me to follow your example and make use of sorrow to remain united to you and your Divine Son Jesus.*

ECAUSE he clung to me, I will deliver him; I will defend him because he has known my name.

APR.
7

—Ps 91:14

REFLECTION. Have devotion to the holy Name of Mary; ask God for it!

Think of this blessed Name and invoke it often with all the respect and veneration it deserves. —*St. John Baptist de la Salle*

PRAYER. *O Mary, grant me a loving devotion to your holy Name. Let me repeat often each day an invocation to it like: "May every age be mindful of your holy Name."*

HRIST . . . gave himself for our sins that he might deliver us from the evil of this age according to the will of our God and Father. —Gal 1:3-4

APR.
8

REFLECTION. The whole world is indebted to Jesus for His Passion.

Similarly, all of us are indebted to our Lady for her compassion. —*St. Albert the Great*

PRAYER. *O Mary, by your union with Christ's sufferings you are our Co-Redemptrix. Let me continually thank you for your compassion, especially by cooperating with all the graces given me each day.*

ECAUSE of the Lord's mercy, we are not consumed, for his compassion never fails. It is renewed each morning. Great is your faithfulness. —Lam 3:22-23

REFLECTION.   Mary offered her Son generously in sacrifice to satisfy the justice of God.

Hence, we can truly say that she cooperated in the salvation of the human race along with Christ. —*Pope Benedict XV*

PRAYER.   *O Mary, in sorrow you still cooperated with the Lord, for you knew that God will never be outdone in generosity. Help me to show my gratitude in action for all that God has done for me.*

BEAR with everything for the sake of the chosen, so that they also may obtain the salvation that is in Christ Jesus, with heavenly glory. —2 Tim 2:10

REFLECTION.   What an exchange! Mary receives John in place of Jesus, the servant in place of the Lord, the disciple in place of the Master.

She receives the son of Zebedee in place of the Son of God, a mere man in place of the true God! —*St. Bernard*

PRAYER.   *O Mary, you bore even the great loss of Jesus in order to obtain salvation for us. Help me to appreciate what a great thing eternal salvation is and to work for it at all times.*

O one hates his own body but rather nourishes and protects it, even as Christ does the Church, for we are members of his body. —Eph 5:29-30

REFLECTION.   All who are united to Christ have issued from the womb of Mary, and she is the Mother of us all.

Who can doubt that she will work most diligently to procure that Christ may transfer His gifts to us, His members, above all the gift of knowing Him and living through Him.

—*St. Pius X*

PRAYER.   *O Mary, you are continually working to lead us more perfectly to your Divine Son. Grant me the grace to know Jesus better and the resolution to live through Him.*

———————

 EARN from me, for I am meek and humble of heart; and you will find rest for your souls. —Mt 11:29

REFLECTION.   I am sure that Mary's actual life must have been a very simple one.

Instead of thinking of her as unapproachable, we must realize how truly imitable she was, how outstanding were her virtues, and how she lived by faith as we do.

—*St. Theresa of Lisieux*

PRAYER.   *O Mary, your life and virtues are a beacon for us in the stormy night of this world. Help me to try to imitate one virtue of yours each day, starting with your blessed simplicity.*

LEARN wisdom, my son, and make me joyful, and I will be able to answer him who taunts me. The prudent see evil and hide. —Prov 27:11-12

APR. 13

REFLECTION. Those who fail to do the works of their Mother renounce their lineage.

Mary is humble, but they are proud. Mary is pure, but they are wicked. Mary is full of love, but they are full of hate for others.

—*St. Peter Chrysologus*

PRAYER. *O Mary, you gave us an example of good works. Help me to follow your good example, not my evil inclinations. Let me root out all that is not Marylike in me.*

AMEN, amen, I say to you . . . , I am the living bread that has come down from heaven; if anyone eats this bread, he will live forever. —Jn 6:47-51

APR. 14

REFLECTION. It is through Mary that we are able to eat the Bread of Heaven every day.

Through her intercession, God inspires us to receive this Bread and confers on us the grace to receive it worthily. —*St. Peter Damian*

PRAYER. *O Mary, you are our Lady of the Eucharist. Help me to participate fully in the Mass as often as possible and receive the Body and Blood, Soul and Divinity of your Son Jesus, in Holy Communion.*

UT flee the desires of youth and seek justice, faith, love, and peace, along with those who call on the Lord from a pure heart. —2 Tim 2:22

APR. 15

REFLECTION. The purer are your words and your glances, the more pleasing will you be to the Blessed Virgin.

And the greater will be the graces that she will obtain for you from her Divine Son.

—*St. John Bosco*

PRAYER. *O Mary, you are the Virgin Most Pure. Obtain for me the grace to preserve purity of mind and heart. Let me avoid the proximate occasions of sin and call upon your help in any difficulty.*

HE Lord loves his foundation on the holy mountains. . . . Glorious things are said of you, O City of God! —Ps 87:2-3

APR. 16

REFLECTION. Mary was foretold by the Prophets and foreshadowed in types and figures by the Patriarchs.

She was described by the Evangelists and saluted most courteously by the Angels.

—*St. Sophronius*

PRAYER. *O Mary, the Scriptures speak volumes about you in types and figures, such as "Judith" and the "City of God." Teach me to learn more about you by searching the Scriptures with a Marian bent.*

ET your eyes look straight forward and your gaze be directly ahead. Make level the path for your feet and let your ways be secure. —Prov 4:25-26

REFLECTION.   God has established Mary as a bridge that leads to salvation.

By making use of this bridge, we pass safely over the stormy sea of this world and reach the happy harbor of heaven.   —*St. James of Nisibis*

PRAYER.   *O Mary, you are our Bridge of Salvation. Let me look only to you to lead me unerringly to your Divine Son. Grant that I may never deviate from your saving guidance.*

———————————

EFORE you I cry in the day and weep in the night. Let my prayer ascend to you; hear my cry of sorrow.

—Ps 88:2-3

REFLECTION.   Nothing assures our perseverance in faith except assiduous prayer to Mary.

But can we pray all the time? I say yes, if we love Mary very much.   —*St. Alphonsus Liguori*

PRAYER.   *O Mary, you are the ensurer of final perseverance. Teach me to pray to you with persistence. Let no day go by that I fail to pray for my earthly well-being and eternal bliss.*

LENGTH of days is in her right hand, and in her left are riches and glory. Her ways are wonderful ways, and all her paths are peaceful. —Prov 3:16-17

APR. 19

REFLECTION.   Live in Mary's heart, love what she loves, and desire what she desires.

Then you are sure to have peace, joy, and holiness. —*St. John Eudes*

PRAYER.   *O Mary, you desire complete union with your children. Help me to consecrate to you my very being and my whole life: all that I have, all that I love, and all that I am.*

———————

THROUGH his torment, my servant shall justify many, and he shall bear their iniquities. . . . For he has borne the sins of many. —Isa 53:11-12

APR. 20

REFLECTION.   When Jesus said the words "Behold your Mother," he meant this:

"My wounds are sources of graces that flow only through Mary." —*St. Andrew of Crete*

PRAYER.   *O Mary, you are the channel of the graces that Jesus won for us by His suffering. Help me to show my gratitude to Jesus, and grant me the graces I need for my state in life.*

WHEN they came to Jesus and saw that he was already dead, they did not break his legs, but one soldier opened his side with a lance, and immediately blood and water poured out. —Jn 19:33-34

REFLECTION. It is your Heart, O Mary, that is pierced with the steel of the lance.

Much more so than the Heart of your Son, Who has already breathed His last. —*St. Bernard*

PRAYER. *O Mary, let me grieve with you over the saving death of your beloved Son. "Holy Mother, pierce me through./ In my heart each wound renew/ of my Savior crucified!"*

───────────

EVERYONE who has left houses, or brothers, or sisters, or father, or mother, or wife, or children, or lands for my name's sake, will receive a hundredfold and will inherit life everlasting. —Mt 19:29

REFLECTION. To other human beings, grace has been given with measure.

But to Mary, it has been poured out beyond measure! —*St. Sophronius*

PRAYER. *O Mary, you are full of grace, possessing more than all the Angels and Saints combined. I bow down in awe at the breadth of your holiness, and I ask you to pray to the all-holy God for me.*

ALL flesh was destroyed that moved upon the earth . . . from man even to beast. . . . Only Noah and those with him in the ark remained.

APR.
23

—Gen 7:21-23

REFLECTION. Noah's ark was a type of Mary. As, by its means, human beings were preserved from the Flood, so are we all saved by Mary from the shipwreck of sin.

There is this difference, however. In the ark few were saved, but through Mary the whole human race was rescued from death.

—*St. Bernard*

PRAYER. *O Mary, you are the Ark of Salvation for all humankind. I entrust to you myself and my family as well as the whole world. Keep us all from eternal death.*

 GREAT is the Lord and worthy of all praise in the city of our God. His holy mountain, most beautiful of all, is the joy of the whole earth.

APR.
24

—Ps 48:2

REFLECTION. Our Lord had preserved the soul together with the body of the Blessed Virgin in that purity which became her who was to receive a God into her womb.

For, as God is holy, He reposes only in holy places.

—*St. John Damascene*

PRAYER. *O Mary, you were given the grace of the highest holiness so as to be able to have God reposing in you. Help me to strive after the greatest holiness possible since your Divine Son dwells in me, too, by grace.*

TRY to please everyone in all things, not
seeking my own good but the good of the
many, that they may be saved. Be imitators of me, as I am of Christ.

APR.
25

—1 Cor 10:33—11:1

REFLECTION.   The Blessed Virgin Mary was the
nearest possible to Christ, for it was from her
that He received His human nature.

Therefore, she must have obtained a greater
plenitude of grace from Him than all others.

—*St. Thomas Aquinas*

PRAYER.   *O Mary, you are the most like Christ
out of all human beings. Help me to imitate
you in every way, for in so doing I will also imitate your Divine Son as closely as possible.*

OR thus says the high and exalted one,
who lives forever, whose name is holy,
who dwells in a lofty, holy place.

APR.
26

—Isa 57:15

REFLECTION.   Let every creature be silent and
tremble and scarcely dare glance at the immensity of so great a dignity.

God dwells in the Blessed Virgin, with whom
He has the identity of one nature.

—*St. Peter Damian*

PRAYER.   *O Mary, how great is your dignity as
the Holy Mother of God! Let me never hesitate
to honor you and to proclaim your greatness to
others by words and works.*

SHOUT and sing for joy, O City of Zion, **APR.** for great is he in your midst, the Holy **27** One of Israel.

—Isa 12:6

REFLECTION. When we say that Mary is the Mother of God, we speak of a dignity that is above every other dignity that can be named, or thought of, after that of God.

Nothing equals Mary, for all is either above her, and this is God, or beneath her, and this is all that is not God. —*St. Anselm*

PRAYER. *O Mary, you are the Virgin Most Venerable, for God alone can know your real greatness. Grant that I may venerate you as you deserve.*

YOU are the glory of Jerusalem, the **APR.** surpassing pride of Israel, the great **28** honor of our people. You have done all this with your own hand.

—Jud 15:9-10

REFLECTION. The Blessed Virgin was united with Jesus in the closest and most indissoluble bond.

Together with Jesus and through Jesus, she was the eternal enemy of the poisonous serpent, overcame him, and crushed his head with her virginal foot. —*Pope Pius IX*

PRAYER. *O Mary, in union with your Divine Son you have overcome the powers of evil. Come to my aid when evil threatens to overwhelm me, and deliver me from all danger.*

UT you are a God of mercy, gracious and compassionate, slow to anger and full of love. Therefore, you did not forsake them. —Neh 9:17

REFLECTION. Have recourse to that dear Mary who is the Mother of Mercy.

She will take you into her Son's presence and use her Motherly intercession with Him on your behalf, so that He will be merciful toward you. —*St. Catherine of Siena .*

PRAYER. *O Mary, Mother of Mercy, never: cease to intercede for me with your merciful Son. Let me remember that all human beings are fallible and I need God's mercy to reach my eternal goal.*

 OU have remitted the guilt of your people; you have forgiven all their sins. You have held back all your wrath; you have not lashed out with anger. —Ps 85:3-4

REFLECTION. Mary, ever Virgin, is a true Mother of Mercy, who disposes Jesus to clemency.

As a consoler of the human race, she never ceases to pour out before Him her prayer for the salvation of the faithful crushed by the weight of their sins. —*St. Pius V*

PRAYER. *O Mary, you continually plead for us before the throne of your Divine Son. Help me to show my gratitude for His mercy toward me by striving to avoid all sin in the future.*

HE is the reflection of eternal light, the spotless mirror of the active power of God, and the image of his goodness.
—Wis 7:26

MAY 1

REFLECTION. Before her birth, the Prophets proclaimed the glory of Mary. They compared her to the sun.

Indeed, the appearances of the Blessed Virgin can be compared to a beautiful ray of sunshine on a cloudy afternoon. —*St. John Vianney*

PRAYER. *O Mary, you are the Sunshine of our lives. Let your rays of grace shine into my heart and cast out the darkness of sin and despair. Let me hope always in you.*

 OME to me, all you who desire me, and eat your fill of my fruits. For the memory of me is sweeter than honey; to possess me is sweeter than the honeycomb.
—Sir 24:18-19

MAY 2

REFLECTION. May the life of Mary, who gave birth to God, be for all of you as instructive as if it were written down.

Come to know yourselves in her and carry out the good works that you have neglected in the past. —*St. Athanasius*

PRAYER. *O Mary, help me to meditate often on your life and to imitate your virtues. In so doing, I will attain a living knowledge of Jesus and the Father—which Jesus said constitutes eternal life.*

PUT bracelets on your hands, a chain about your neck, . . . earrings in your ears, and a shining crown upon your head. **MAY 3** —Ezek 16:11-12

REFLECTION. How beautiful you are in soul and resplendent in body, Mary, my Mother.

In this world, the Blessed Virgin was poor and unknown, but in heaven she is glorious and beautiful, the Queen of Angels.

—*St. Anthony of Padua*

PRAYER. *O Mary, you are all beautiful in both soul and body. I praise you as the Queen of heaven and earth. Let me appreciate your beauty and spiritual might ever more each day.*

———————

 LL these blessings shall come upon you and overtake you if you hear [God's] precepts. . . . And blessed shall you be coming in and going out. **MAY 4** —Deut 28:2-6

REFLECTION. Entrust to Mary any offering you wish to make to God. In this way, grace will return to its source the same way it came to us.

Certainly, God could give us grace without going through Mary. But He chose not to do so.

—*St. Bernard*

PRAYER. *O Mary, grant me the graces God intends for me this day. Then offer to your Divine Son all the good works that I do as a result of these graces.*

GLAD heart makes a cheerful face, but by grief of mind the spirit is broken. The wise of heart seek knowledge. **MAY 5** —Prov 15:13-14

REFLECTION. The most holy Heart of Mary is the treasure of holiness, the furnace of Divine Love, the throne of all virtues, and the sanctuary of the Trinity.

May that Heart be forever blessed and celebrated throughout the universe! —*St. John Eudes*

PRAYER. *O Immaculate Heart of Mary, may my heart be ever united with yours. Grant that I may hate sin, love God and my neighbor, and reach eternal life together with those I love.*

 HO is she that comes forth like the dawn, fair as the moon, bright as the sun, majestic as an army in battle array? **MAY 6** —SS 6:10

REFLECTION. Mary is more exalted than the Patriarchs, greater than the Martyrs, more glorious than the Confessors, and purer than the Virgins.

Therefore, she alone and without them can do what they can accomplish only in union with her. —*St. Anselm*

PRAYER. *O Mary, your Divine Son has placed His own mighty power into your hands. By that power, help me to flee all sin and practice my faith conscientiously day after day.*

THUS do I look up to you . . . that I may behold your power and your glory. For your kindness is better than life; my lips shall proclaim your praises. —Ps 63:3-4

REFLECTION. In Mary's name, I say this to each one of you:

She loves you, each and every one of you. She loves you very much. She loves you at every moment and without any exceptions.

—*St. Maximilian Kolbe*

PRAYER. *O Mary, I offer you deep thanks for your great love for all those redeemed by your Divine Son. Help me to respond to that love by loving my neighbor for the love of you and Jesus.*

_____

HE can do all things; while unchanging herself, she makes all things new. Generation after generation she enters into holy souls, and turns them into friends of God and prophets. —Wis 7:27

REFLECTION. We have recourse to Mary in prayer because she is by the side of God's throne as Mediatrix of Divine Grace.

Most acceptable to God by worthiness and by merit, Mary is more powerful than all the Angels and Saints in heaven. —*Pope Leo XIII*

PRAYER. *O Mary, inspire me to come to you in all my difficulties. Help me to be ever devoted to you and to receive the graces I need to be with you and your Divine Son in heaven.*

THE mother of the sons of Zebedee came to [Jesus] . . . and worshiping him, asked for a favor. He said to her, "What is your wish?" —Mt 20:20-21

MAY 9

REFLECTION. When Mary asks for graces from God, she does not ask but, so to speak, commands.

For her Son honors her by refusing her nothing. —*St. Peter Damian*

PRAYER. *O most powerful Advocate, "help the helpless, strengthen the fearful, comfort the sorrowful, pray for the people, plead for the clergy, intercede for all women consecrated to God, and assist all those devoted to you."*

———————

LL my words are just; in them is no evil or wickedness. They are right to those who understand.
—Prov 8:8-9

MAY 10

REFLECTION. What a wondrous book is the Heart of Mary!

Blessed are those who read with intelligence what is written therein, for they will learn the science of salvation. —*St. John Eudes*

PRAYER. *O Mary most wise, help me to contemplate the science of salvation found in your Immaculate Heart. Grant that I may imitate you in all things, for you were the perfect follower of Jesus.*

BELOVED, we are the children of God now; what we shall be has not yet appeared. We do know that when he appears, we shall be like him. —1 Jn 3:2

MAY 11

REFLECTION.   Mary is the living "mold of God." It was in her that God was made a true man.

It is also in her that human beings can be truly fashioned into God, insofar as that is possible for human nature, by the grace of Christ.

—*St. Louis Grignion de Montfort*

PRAYER.   *O Mary, you are the mold of Christ. Form us into the image of your Divine Son. Help me to be like Jesus, so that I may be forever a true child of God.*

MARY . . . shall bring forth a son and you shall call his name Jesus, because he shall save his people from their sins.   —Mt 1:20-21

MAY 12

REFLECTION.   By becoming the Mother of God, Mary was the means of the salvation of sinners.

In the same way, sinners are saved by proclaiming her praises.   —*St. Anselm*

PRAYER.   *O Mary, you are the Refuge of Sinners. Help me to receive the Sacrament of Penance worthily, so that my sins will be forgiven and I will sing your praises forever.*

CRY to you from the ends of the earth when my heart becomes weary. You will set me high on a rock giving me rest, for you are my refuge. —Ps 61:3-4

MAY 13

REFLECTION. If you wish to live supernaturally and holily, pray to the Mother of God.

When you see yourself becoming lost in activity, make contact with our Immaculate Mother by frequent interior appeals.

—*St. Maximilian Kolbe*

PRAYER. *O Mary, you always listen to our prayers. Help me to remain united with you in prayer despite the many activities that cry for my attention at every moment of the day.*

———————

 ND Mary said: "My soul magnifies the Lord; and my spirit rejoices in God my savior."

MAY 14

—Lk 1:46-47

REFLECTION. May each one of us possess the soul of Mary to proclaim the greatness of the Lord.

And may each one of us possess the spirit of Mary to rejoice in God. —*St. Ambrose*

PRAYER. *O Mary, you magnified the Lord by your life as well as your words. Obtain for me the grace to glorify the Lord and rejoice in Him by the purity of my life.*

AN a woman forget her infant, be without mercy for the child of her womb? And if she should forget, I shall never forget you. —Isa 49:15

MAY 15

REFLECTION. The Blessed Virgin Mary is like a mother who has many children.

She is always busy going from one to the other! —*St. John Vianney*

PRAYER. *O Mary, you are more devoted to the salvation of your children than any earthly mother can be. I thank you for your loving concern for me, which will only rest when I am in heaven with you.*

ARY kept in mind all these things, pondering them in her heart. Then the shepherds returned, glorifying and lauding God for all they had heard and seen. —Lk 2:19-20

MAY 16

REFLECTION. O faithful soul, imitate the Blessed Virgin Mary.

Enter into the temple of your heart in order to be spiritually renewed and obtain forgiveness of your sins. Remember that God looks at the intentions behind our works rather than the works themselves. —*St. Lawrence Justinian*

PRAYER. *O Mary, you meditated continually on the things God sent into your life. Help me to meditate daily on the events that touch my life and to discern God's hand and will in them.*

T that time, Mary arose and went into the hill country in haste to a town of Judah. She entered the home of Zechariah and greeted Elizabeth.

MAY 17

—Lk 1:39-40

REFLECTION. In the interior life and in the apostolate, let us always work with Mary.

For then everything becomes easier and more certain, quicker and more delightful.

—*St. Louis Grignion de Montfort*

PRAYER. *O Mary, you were forever working for the Christian apostolate. Teach me to work with you so that I may obtain the best fruits from this activity, which Jesus commanded us to do.*

NYTHING defiled shall not enter into it nor anyone who practices abomination and deceit, but only those who appear in the book of life of the Lamb.

MAY 18

—Rev 21:27

REFLECTION. Those who enjoy the favor of Mary are recognized by the citizens of heaven.

And those who bear her stamp, that is, those who have the grace to be her servants, are inscribed in the Book of Life.

—*St. Bonaventure*

PRAYER. *O Mary, you are the Book of Life for your servants. Help me to be so devoted to you that I will remain free from serious sin and deserve to have my name written in that Book.*

WOMAN from the crowd cried out . . . , "Blessed is the womb that bore you. . . ." He replied, "Rather, blessed are those who hear the word of God and obey it."

—Lk 11:27-28

REFLECTION. Mary is blessed most of all because she heard the word of God and carried it out.

She preserved the Truth in her mind even more than she preserved the Flesh in her womb. —*St. Augustine*

PRAYER. *O Mary, you are the first among the believers in Christ. Increase my faith in your Divine Son. Make it so alive that it will shine out even in the littlest thing I do.*

ET us confidently draw near the throne of grace to receive mercy and to find grace to help in time of need.

—Heb 4:16

REFLECTION. The life-giving graces flow from Christ the Head, through the Blessed Virgin, into His Mystical Body.

Mary received the great honor from God that no one should obtain any grace except through her hands. —*St. Bernardine*

PRAYER. *O Mary, you are the Mediatrix of all graces. Let me ask you each day for the graces I need to lead a truly Christian life, and obtain them for me from your Divine Son.*

SHE is found by those who search for her. She hastens to make herself known to those who desire her; those who rise early to seek her will not have to toil.

MAY 21

—Wis 6:12-14

REFLECTION. The Blessed Virgin is invoked in the Church under the titles of Advocate, Auxiliatrix, Adjutrix, and Mediatrix.

These however are to be so understood that they take nothing away from nor add anything to the dignity and efficacy of Christ the one Mediator. —*Vatican II, The Church, 62*

PRAYER. *O Mary, you are our Advocate with God. Grant that I may call upon your intercessory power and so be able to bring forth the fruits that your Divine Son expects from me.*

LORD, . . . you have been pleased to bless the house of your servant, so that it will always remain. It is you, O Lord, who blessed it, and it will be blessed forever. — 1 Chr 17:26-27

MAY 22

REFLECTION. Without the consent of Mary, God would not become Man.

The reasons for this were first that we might feel under great obligation to her and second that we might realize that the salvation of all is left to her care. —*St. Peter Damian*

PRAYER. *O Mary, you are entrusted with our salvation. Keep me safe from the snares of the devil. Help me to say often: "Immaculate Heart of Mary, be my salvation."*

HE has set her table. She has sent out her maids to invite to the tower . . . : "Let whoever is a little one come to me." —Prov 9:2-4

MAY 23

REFLECTION. Nowhere do we find Jesus nearer to us and more adapted to our weakness than in Mary, since it was for that reason that He came and dwelt in her.

Everywhere else He is the Bread of the strong, the Bread of the Angels, but in Mary He is the Bread of children.

—*St. Louis Grignion de Montfort*

PRAYER. *O Mary, you bring Jesus to us in a way we can understand. Let me come to know Jesus more deeply, love Him more dearly, and follow Him more closely.*

 OPE does not disappoint, because the charity of God is poured forth in our hearts through the Holy Spirit who has been given to us. —Rom 5:5

MAY 24

REFLECTION. The Holy Spirit is all the love of the Blessed Trinity, and Mary is all the love of Creation.

In their union, heaven is united with earth, the whole of eternal Love with the whole of created love. It constitutes the zenith of love!

—*St. Maximilian Kolbe*

PRAYER. *O Mary, you bring us the love of God through the Holy Spirit. Make me acutely aware of the Holy Spirit and grant me the grace to follow His promptings and grow in His love.*

BUT if anyone sins, we have an advocate with God the Father, Jesus Christ the just one. He is propitiation for our sins . . . and those of all the world.

MAY
25

—1 Jn 2:1-2

REFLECTION.   In heaven Mary remains always in the presence of her Divine Son.

There she is continually praying on behalf of sinners.   —*St. Bede the Venerable*

PRAYER.   *O Mary, in accord with the will of your Divine Son, you are the Refuge of Sinners. Beg Him to forgive my past sins and help me to avoid sin in the future.*

THE just shall hold to his way, and whoever has clean hands shall grow ever stronger.

MAY
26

—Job 17:9

REFLECTION.   My children, do you want to obtain perseverance?

Then be devoted to our Blessed Lady!

—*St. Philip Neri*

PRAYER.   *O Mary, you obtain the grace of final perseverance for your children. Help me to be a devoted child of yours, so that I may remain in the state of grace until death and join you with your Son in heaven.*

FOR you were slain and have redeemed us for God with your blood, those from every tribe and language, people and nation. —Rev 5:9

REFLECTION. God is the Father of the world's construction, and Mary is the Mother of its reconstruction.

For God generated the One through Whom everything has been made. And Mary gave birth to the One through Whose work all things have been saved. —*St. Anselm*

PRAYER. *O Mary, you are the Co-Redemptrix with your Divine Son. Help me to unite all my words and actions with your Heart and the Sacred Heart of Jesus for the salvation of the world.*

ABIDE in me, and I in you. . . . Whoever abides in me and I in him will bear much fruit, for without me you can do nothing. —Jn 15:4-5

REFLECTION. It was the prerogative of Mary to conceive Christ in her womb.

But it is the heritage of all the elect to bear Jesus in their hearts. —*St. Peter Damian*

PRAYER. *O Mary, you bore Christ in your heart as well as your body. Help me to bear Him always within my heart by doing the things that are pleasing to Him.*

H EAR me, daughter, do not glean in any other field. . . . Keep close to my maids and follow where they glean.
—Ru 2:8-9

REFLECTION.   Like Ruth Mary is allowed to gather the ears of corn (glean) after harvesters.

The harvesters she follows are all evangelical laborers constantly harvesting souls for God. To Mary alone is granted to save the most hardened sinners, abandoned even by the harvesters.   —*St. Bonaventure*

PRAYER.   *O Mary, you intercede even for the most hardened souls. Convert the most rebellious and bring them back to Jesus.*

H EAR now, all you who fear God, and I will tell you the great things he has done for me. I cried to him for help, and praised him with my tongue.
—Ps 66:16-17

REFLECTION.   Every day at Evening Prayer, the Church sings the "Magnificat," Mary's hymn of praise.

This habitual remembrance of the Lord's Incarnation enkindles the hearts of the faithful, and the frequent meditation of Mary's examples confirms them in virtue.   —*St. Bede*

PRAYER.   *O Mary, teach me to unite myself with the Church in the Liturgy of the Hours each day. Let me recite your magnificent hymn of praise often.*

ARY stayed with Elizabeth about three months and then returned to her own home.

—Lk 1:56

MAY
31

REFLECTION. The heart of our good Mother Mary is all love and mercy. She desires nothing else but our happiness.

We need only have recourse to her and we will be heard. —*St. John Vianney*

PRAYER. *O Mary, you visited Elizabeth on a mission of mercy even while bearing Jesus. Teach me to be concerned for others and bring Jesus to them by my visits.*

———————

TORE up treasures for yourselves in heaven, where neither moth nor rust consumes, nor robbers break in and steal! For where your treasure is, there also will your heart be.

—Mt 6:20-21

JUNE
1

REFLECTION. Mary is my great treasure. She is my All after Jesus.

She is my honor, my tenderness, and the storehouse of my virtues! I do everything in and through her. —*St. Louis Grignion de Montfort*

PRAYER. *O Mary, you are our greatest treasure after Jesus. Help me to prize you above everything, remain united with you, and reach your Son Jesus through you.*

YOU shall search for me, and you shall find me, when you seek me with all your heart. I will be found by you, and I will bring you back. —Jer 29:13-14

JUNE 2

REFLECTION. We must pray to Mary and call upon her. She is admirable for herself and lovable for us.

As in the Gospel, Mary now intervenes with her Son and obtains from Him miracles that the ordinary course of things would not allow.

—*Pope Paul VI*

PRAYER. *O Mary, you know our human needs and sorrows. Grant that I may have recourse to you in all my anxieties and always obtain God's gracious help.*

———————

I BECAME established in Zion. Thus, in the beloved city he gave me a resting place; in Jerusalem I wield my power. —Sir 24:10-11

JUNE 3

REFLECTION. The word "Jerusalem" in this text signifies the Church Triumphant in heaven as well as the Church Militant on earth.

Indeed, the Mother of the Creator has power both in heaven and on earth. —*St. Bonaventure*

PRAYER. *O Mary, you are the "Virgin Most Powerful." Make me a better person and make the world a safer place to live in from both a natural and a supernatural point of view.*

MERCY and truth shall meet; justice and peace shall kiss. Truth shall sprout from the earth, and justice shall look down from heaven.

JUNE 4

—Ps 85:11-12

REFLECTION. Mary is the Virgin most truthful, the soil from which, in the words of the Psalmist, Truth shall spring.

May she grant us the grace to be truthful in heart, word, and deed in all things.

—*St. Joan of Valois*

PRAYER. *O Mary, you are the Mother of Truth Himself. Make me know the Truth, so that I may always love the truth, speak the truth, and live the truth.*

DO not be anxious and say, "What shall we eat?" or "What shall we drink?" or "What shall we wear?" ... All these things shall be given you besides.

JUNE 5

—Mt 6:31-33

REFLECTION. Place yourself in Mary's hands; she will think of everything and provide for the needs of soul and body.

Therefore, be at peace, be at complete peace, with unlimited confidence in her!

—*St. Maximilian Kolbe*

PRAYER. *O Mary, Mother of Hope, I entrust my life into your hands. Fill me with Christian optimism, so that I will be able to confront any situation with equanimity.*

ASSOCIATE with a devout person whom you know to be a keeper of the commandments. . . . In addition, trust your own judgment.

JUNE
6

—Sir 37:12-13

REFLECTION. Jesus has given us the Heart of His Blessed Mother. Therefore, you can and you must make use of that Heart to love God.

For Mary's Heart is truly yours, and you must love God with all your heart! —*St. John Eudes*

PRAYER. *O Immaculate Heart of Mary, I entrust myself to you. Help me to follow your inspirations and make my heart like yours, which is in turn like the Heart of Jesus.*

———————

FOR those who observe the holy precepts with holiness will be accounted holy. . . . Therefore, be zealous in heeding my words; long for them and you will receive instruction. —Wis 6:10-11

JUNE
7

REFLECTION. Mary is the sure way to go to Jesus and to find Him perfectly.

It is through her that holy souls, who are to radiate holiness, must find Jesus!

—*St. Louis Grignion de Montfort*

PRAYER. *O Mary, you lead us unfailingly to Jesus. Help me to follow your inspirations in all things and to radiate your Divine Son to the whole world.*

ISTEN, my people, to my teaching; incline your ears to the words of my mouth. I will open my mouth to speak parables, I will reveal mysteries of long ago.
—Ps 78:1-2

REFLECTION.   Mary is the vessel and tabernacle containing all mysteries. All that was hidden from preceding generations was made known to her.

Even more, most of the wonders of the Divine plan of salvation depended on her.
—*St. Gregory the Wonderworker*

PRAYER.   *O Mary, help me to realize that like you every person has a role in God's saving plan. Grant that I may fulfill my role, no matter how difficult it may be.*

NOTHER angel came and stood before the altar, with a golden censer. . . . And with the prayers of the saints, the cloud of incense rose up before God from the angel's hand.
—Rev 8:3-4

REFLECTION.   The incomparable Mother of God is the purest golden censer.

In her our prayers are offered to the Eternal God.
—*St. Ephrem*

PRAYER.   *O Mary, you present our prayers to God without ceasing. Beg your Divine Son to forgive me my sins so that I may offer prayers to Him forever in heaven.*

IF you, evil as you are, know how to give good things to your children, how much more will your Father in heaven give good things to those who ask him! —Mt 7:11

JUNE 10

REFLECTION. Everything that the Son asks of the Father is granted.

Likewise, everything that the Mother asks of her Son is also granted. —*St. John Vianney*

PRAYER. *O Mary, as our loving Mother you have our happiness at heart. Inspire me to ask only for those things that will further God's glory and the salvation of souls, including my own.*

———————

THE eyes of all hope in you . . . ; you open your hand and satisfy the desire of every living thing. —Ps 145:15-16

JUNE 11

REFLECTION. The Motherly Heart of Mary has a great desire to give us grace.

This desire is even greater than our desire to receive grace! —*St. Alphonsus Liguori*

PRAYER. *O Mary, you are forever looking for ways to give us grace. Grant me the grace I need for this day, and let me remember to ask for the same thing each day.*

BSERVE . . . the commandment . . . : love the Lord, your God; walk in all his ways; keep all his commandments; cling to him; and serve him with all your heart and soul.—Jos 22:5

JUNE 12

REFLECTION.   Love the Immaculata! Confide in her and consecrate yourself to her without reservation.

Strive to do everything as she herself would do it in your place, especially by loving God as she loves Him.   —*St. Maximilian Kolbe*

PRAYER.   *O Mary, I give myself completely to you. Help me to love you, to follow your example in all things, and to love God as you did all your life.*

―――――――――

UT now that you are free from sin and slaves to God, the fruit that you have leads to holiness and results in eternal life.   —Rom 6:22

JUNE 13

REFLECTION.   Blessed are those who cherish your Name, O Mary.

Your favor will sustain them in the midst of trials, and they will bring forth fruits of salvation.   —*St. Anthony of Padua*

PRAYER.   *O Mary, may your holy Name be ever on my lips and in my heart. Let it be the key to a good life on earth and the password to a blessed eternity in heaven.*

WISDOM is sweet for your soul. If you find it, you will have hope, and your hope will not perish.
—Prov 24:14

JUNE
14

REFLECTION.   Mary is both the Mother of the Shepherd and the Mother of the Lamb.

That is why she is all our confidence and all our hope!
—*St. Germanus*

PRAYER.   *O Mary, you are the world's best hope because you are the Mother of the Redeemer. I place all my hope in you—for today, for tomorrow, and for ever.*

COME and let us reason together . . . : If your sins are like scarlet, they may become as white as snow. And if they are red as crimson, they may become as white as wool.
—Isa 1:18

JUNE
15

REFLECTION.   The greater sinners we are, the more tenderness and compassion Mary has for us.

The child who has cost the Mother the most tears is closest to her heart!
—*St. John Vianney*

PRAYER.   *O Mary, you are full of compassion for us. If I should ever have the misfortune to fall into serious sin, help me to throw myself upon your loving mercy.*

AY the Lord guide your hearts to the love of God and to the perseverance of Christ.

JUNE 16

—2 Thes 3:5

REFLECTION. The love of Christ so wounded and transfixed Mary's Heart that no part of it remained untouched.

Thus, she fulfilled the First Commandment in all its extension and without the slightest imperfection. —*St. Bernard*

PRAYER. *O Mary, your love for God is greater than the love of all human beings together. Teach me to love God with all my heart, all my mind, and all my soul.*

HO do you think is the faithful and prudent steward whom the master will put in charge of his household to give them food ? . . . Blessed is that servant whom his master finds doing so when he arrives home.

JUNE 17

—Lk 12:42-43

REFLECTION. We have only one thing that we must do—that is, pray to the Blessed Virgin.

Ask her for the grace to love our Lord as she loves Him and to remain faithful to Him in life and in death. —*St. Bernadette*

PRAYER. *O Mary, you are the Virgin Most Faithful. Grant me the grace to love God and remain faithful to Him in all things.*

BEING rooted and grounded in love, may you come to comprehend . . . what is the breadth, length, height and depth, and to know the love of Christ that surpasses all understanding.

JUNE 18

—Eph 3:17-19

REFLECTION. Do you wish to know the most intimate perfections of Jesus and the most hidden attractions of His love?

Then seek them in the Heart of Mary!

—*St. Peter Eymard*

PRAYER. *O Mary, keep ever before me the tried and trusted Christian motto: "To Jesus through Mary." And let me learn to seek your Divine Son in your Motherly Heart.*

———————

THEY cried out to you, and from heaven you heard them and rescued them according to your compassion time after time.

JUNE 19

—Neh 9:28

REFLECTION. Mary is not only *called* the Mother of Mercy. She *is* the Mother of Mercy.

And she proved that she is by the loving tenderness with which she helps us all.

—*St. Alphonsus Liguori*

PRAYER. *O Mary, you are the Mother of Mercy. Plead my cause day and night before your Divine Son. In your mercy, do not let me be lost forever.*

PHILIP said to him, "Master, show us the Father, and that is enough for us." Jesus said to him, ". . . Whoever sees me sees also the Father."

—Jn 14:8-9

REFLECTION.   It is the nature of Jesus Christ to lead us surely to the Father.

In the same way, it is the nature of the Blessed Virgin to lead us surely to Jesus.

—*St. Louis Grignion de Montfort*

PRAYER.   *O Mary, you are our sure guide to Jesus. Let me learn to see you in Jesus and Jesus in you. For you are united with your Divine Son by the closest natural and supernatural bond.*

———————

I EXHORT you, therefore, . . . by the mercy of God, to offer your bodies as a sacrifice, living, holy, and delightful, to God, your spiritual service.

—Rom 12:1

REFLECTION.   O holy Mary, into your safe keeping I entrust my soul and body, this day, every day, and on the day of my death.

Through your holy intercession, may all my actions be ordered according to your will and that of your Divine Son.   —*St. Aloysius Gonzaga*

PRAYER.   *O Mary, in accord with the example of St. Aloysius, I offer you this day all my hopes and consolations, all my trials and miseries, my life and the end of my life!*

LET us draw near with a sincere heart and in fullness of trust, with our hearts cleansed from an evil conscience . . . and our bodies cleansed in pure water.

—Heb 10:22

**JUNE
22**

REFLECTION. We must have frequent recourse to the Mother of God for she is the Mother of the supernatural life and the Mother of grace.

The Lord desires that we receive all graces through her, and this depends on our approaching her. —*St. Maximilian Kolbe*

PRAYER. *O Mary, you are the Mother of Divine Grace. Help me to approach you daily with a clean heart to obtain the graces God wishes to give me through you each day.*

———————

AND I heard the voices of many angels around the throne. . . . They numbered thousands upon thousands, and they sang out loudly.

—Rev 5:11

**JUNE
23**

REFLECTION. The nine choirs of Angels offer Mary millions of times each day the Angelic Salutation: Hail Mary!

In doing so, they ask her to honor them with one of her commands.

—*St. Louis Grignion de Montfort*

PRAYER. *O Mary, you are the Queen of Angels. Let me say the "Hail Mary" every day and help me to carry out your commands received through my Guardian Angel.*

THE Lord is joined to you and chose you ... because the Lord loved you and because he kept the oath he had sworn. —Deut 7:7-8

JUNE 24

REFLECTION. What treasure is superior to the Divine Love that animated the Heart of Mary?

It is from this Heart, as from a furnace of Divine Love, that the Blessed Virgin drew forth words of a most ardent love.

—*St. Bernardine of Siena*

PRAYER. *O Mary, you are filled with God's love. Obtain for me a share in that Divine Love so that it may inspire me to love God as much as I am able.*

ET me see your face, let me hear your voice, for your voice is sweet, and your face beautiful. —SS 2:14

JUNE 25

REFLECTION. Come, let us throw ourselves at the feet of this good Mother.

Let us cling to them and not leave them, until she blesses us and takes us for her children.

—*St. Bernard*

PRAYER. *O Mary, you are the best of Mothers. I desire to be your child. Help me to remain ever close to you by following the teachings of your Divine Son.*

I F you search her out and follow her trail, she will make herself known; and once you have found her, do not let her go.

JUNE
26

—Sir 6:27

REFLECTION. Breathing is not only the sign but even the very cause of life.

In like manner, the Name of Mary, continually on the lips of her clients, not only proves the presence of supernatural life but also causes and preserves it and gives them strength for everything. —*St. Germanus*

PRAYER. *O Mary, grant that your holy Name may be always on my lips and in my heart. May it keep me from sin and preserve the Divine life that comes to me from Jesus through you.*

ILL God really dwell with men on earth? If the heavens, even the highest heavens, cannot contain you, how much less this temple that I have built! —1 Ki 8:27

JUNE
27

REFLECTION. The Mother of God contained the infinite God under her Heart, the God Whom no space can contain.

Through her, the Trinity is adored, demons are vanquished, Satan is cast out of heaven, and our fallen nature is assumed into heaven.

—*St. Cyril of Alexandria*

PRAYER. *O Mary, I revere you, who contained within you the God Whom no space can contain. Help me to be ever conscious of God's presence in me through the grace of Jesus.*

BUT to those who did receive [the Redeemer] he gave power to become children of God, to those who believe in his name.
—Jn 1:12

JUNE 28

REFLECTION. Since the Redeemer preexisted, there had to be someone to be saved so that He would not come in vain.

As a consequence, we find Mary, the obedient Virgin, saying: "Behold, I am the handmaid of the Lord. May it be done to me according to your word."
—*St. Irenaeus*

PRAYER. *O Mary, you are the First among the Redeemed and you cooperated in the Redemption. Help me to cooperate in bringing the fruits of Jesus' Redemption to all people.*

YOU have come to him with rich blessings, you have placed on his head a crown of purest gold. . . . For you have made him blessed forever.
—Ps 21:4-7

JUNE 29

REFLECTION. The Name of Mary is second in blessings only to the Most Sacred Name of Jesus.

There is no other name in heaven or on earth that brings such grace, and hope, and sweetness to the devout.
—*St. Alphonsus Liguori*

PRAYER. *O Mary, your Name brings God's blessings to us. Let me pronounce your Name frequently and with loving confidence, so that I too may enjoy the blessings it confers.*

O not urge me to leave you and depart from you. For where you go I will go, where you dwell I will dwell.

—Ru 1:16

JUNE
30

REFLECTION. Ruth, whose name means "seeing and hastening," was a figure of Mary.

For Mary, seeing our miseries, mercifully hastens to help us! —*St. Bonaventure*

PRAYER. *O Mary, like Ruth you remain firmly attached to your people, those redeemed by your Divine Son. See my miseries and make haste to help me.*

F you abide in me and my words abide in you, ask whatever you will and it shall be given you. —Jn 15:7

JULY
1

REFLECTION. Living in Mary means to love Mary with all our heart.

It means to love Mary so much that we are able to live as if we truly inhabited her Immaculate Heart. —*St. Louis Grignion de Montfort*

PRAYER. *O Mary, those who live in you live also in your Divine Son Jesus. Help me to live every moment in you so that I may live forever with Jesus and you in heaven.*

OF his fullness we have all received, one grace after another. For the Law was given through Moses; grace and truth came through Jesus Christ. —Jn 1:16-17

JULY 2

REFLECTION. Our Lord Jesus Christ has obtained for us a magnificent treasure of graces.

But in the Divine Plan, not one particle comes to us without the mediation of Mary.

—*Pope Leo XIII*

PRAYER. *O Mary, no one receives any favor except through you. Help me to ask you each day for the graces I need to remain faithful in my state of life.*

WHOEVER feeds on me will hunger for more; whoever drinks of me will thirst for more. Those who obey me will never be put to shame; those who follow my instructions will never sin. —Sir 24:20-21

JULY 3

REFLECTION. I am sure you do not want to experience any refusal on God's part toward you.

Then do not offer Him anything—neither good works nor prayers—without entrusting them into the hands of Mary. —*St. Bernard*

PRAYER. *O Mary, you are our unfailing intercessor with God. I offer all my good works this day through your hands to your Divine Son Jesus.*

Y faithfulness and my mercy shall be with him, and in my name shall his horn be exalted.

JULY 4

—Ps 89:25

REFLECTION. The Name of Mary refreshes her devoted clients.

It is music to their ears, honey in their mouths, and joy for their hearts.

—*St. Anthony of Padua.*

PRAYER. *O Mary, your holy name is great and brings us salvation. Let me strive to speak it with true love, boundless joy, and complete confidence.*

———————

EACH me judgment and knowledge, for I believe in your commands. . . . I keep your word.

JULY 5

—Ps 119:66-67

REFLECTION. If we look to Mary in all circumstances, we will immediately receive wise inspirations:

Be patient, kind, charitable; comport yourself well, suffer voluntarily, and offer your pains to the Lord. Hope and love always, and give your life authentic Christian meaning.

—*Pope Paul VI*

PRAYER. *O Mary, you are our Mother and our Teacher, instructing us in how to live. Help me to heed your inspirations and follow your Divine Son more closely.*

NTER by the narrow gate. . . . How narrow is the gate and difficult is the road that leads to life. —Mt 7:13-14

JULY 6

REFLECTION. We cannot enter a house without speaking to the doorkeeper.

The Blessed Virgin is the Doorkeeper of Heaven, and we cannot gain entry there without calling upon her help. —*St. John Vianney*

PRAYER. *O Mary, you are the entry for all into heaven. Let me call upon your help frequently on earth, so that when I come you will quickly open heaven's door for me.*

———————

OREVER will I bless your name. Every day I will praise you, and I will extol your name forever and ever.

JULY 7

—Ps 145: 1-2

REFLECTION. The Name of Mary contains within itself the brilliance of the virtues, the sweet refulgence of modesty, and the sacrifice that is pleasing to God.

It is the sign of hospitality and the center of holiness. —*St. Francis Xavier*

PRAYER. *O Mary, I want to be wholly devoted to your Holy Name. Grant that I may invoke it in both good times and bad with ardent love and endless praise.*

NYONE who does not carry his cross and follow me is not worthy of me. . . . Whoever finds his life will lose it, and whoever lays down his life for my sake will find it. —Mt 10:38-39

JULY 8

REFLECTION. Our Lady desires that we not only work for her but also suffer for her.

We must calmly bear the little crosses of each day and even desire that they exist!

—*St. Maximilian Kolbe*

PRAYER. *O Mary, help me to carry my daily crosses in union with you. "Let me share with you His pain,/Who for all our sins was slain,/Who for me in torments died."*

HOEVER entrusts himself to her will possess her, and his descendants will also inherit her. . . . Then [she will] bring him happiness, and reveal her secrets to him. —Sir 4:16-18

JULY 9

REFLECTION. See the confidence that the Church places in Mary.

In all public calamities she invariably calls upon the faithful to enlist her protection through novenas, through prayers and processions, and through visits to her churches and shrines. —*St. Alphonsus Liguori*

PRAYER. *O Mary, the whole Church puts her trust in you. Teach me to trust you completely in all the troubles and adversities of life— whether of body or of soul.*

GRACE and peace be to you from God our Father and from the Lord Jesus Christ.

JULY

10

—Rom 1:7

REFLECTION.   Mary gave being and life to the Author of all grace.

That is why she is called the Mother of Grace.   —*St. Louis Grignion de Montfort*

PRAYER.   *O Mary, you are the Mother of Grace, which is the life of God in us. Obtain from your Divine Son the grace I need as well as the grace sorely needed by the Church and the world.*

AMEN, I say to you, if you have faith and do not doubt, . . . whatever you ask for in prayer believing, you will receive.

JULY

11

—Mt 21:21-22

REFLECTION.   There are many graces that we will not obtain if we ask them of God.

But if we ask them of Mary, we will obtain them, not because she is more powerful but because God wants to honor her in this way.

—*St. Anselm*

PRAYER.   *O Mary, increase my faith in the power that your Divine Son has given you. Grant me the grace to be a true follower of Jesus all the days of my life and sing your glory forever in heaven.*

ITH your goods . . . you satisfied many peoples; with your great wealth . . . you endowed the kings of the earth. —Ezek 27:33

JULY 12

REFLECTION. All the gifts and graces that we receive from God are dispensed by the hands of Mary.

They are given to whom she pleases, when she pleases, and as she pleases.

—*St Bernardine of Siena*

PRAYER. *O Mary, you are most generous with the spiritual gifts entrusted to your care. Make me one of your chosen who receive your gifts eagerly and put them to use diligently in their lives.*

———————————

 IKE a vessel of beaten gold, embellished with every kind of precious stone; like an olive tree laden with fruit, like a cypress reaching to the clouds. . . . —Sir 50:9-10

JULY 13

REFLECTION. The Virgin Mary is like a "vessel" because of her humility.

She is made of "gold" because of her poverty and "embellished with every kind of precious stone" because of her virginity.

—*St. Anthony of Padua*

PRAYER. *O Mary, you are the model of humility, poverty, and virginity. Let me fashion my life after you, so that I will be truly humble, poor in spirit, and pure of heart.*

REFLECT on the decrees of the Lord, and constantly meditate on his commandments. He will enlighten your mind, and the wisdom you desire will be granted to you. —Sir 6:37

JULY 14

REFLECTION. Beneath the light and heat of the sun, plants flourish on earth and bring forth fruit.

Beneath the radiant inspirations of the sun that is Mary, good thoughts flourish in souls.

—*Pope Pius XII*

PRAYER. *O Mary, you are the inspirer of good thoughts in us. Let me dwell on you and on your Divine Son, so that I may always do the things that are pleasing to Jesus.*

THE Lord went before them by day in a pillar of cloud to lead the way. . . . The pillar of cloud never failed to be before the people.

—Ex 13:21-22

JULY 15

REFLECTION. Mary is our "pillar of cloud."

She protects us against the burning rays of the Divine wrath and the fire of temptations.

—*St. Bonaventure*

PRAYER. *O Mary, you are our unceasing protector day and night. Be my aid in all temptations and help me remain truly faithful to my calling, my Church, and my God.*

AY your ear pay attention, and your eyes be focused, to heed the prayer that I, your servant, now offer before you day and night for your people. —Neh 1:6

REFLECTION.   The Hail Mary is the most beautiful of all prayers after the Our Father and the most beautiful compliment you can give to Mary.

It is by this compliment that you will also win her heart, if you say it as you ought.

—*St. Louis Grignion de Montfort*

PRAYER.   *Hail Mary, full of grace, the Lord is with you. Blessed are you among women, and blessed is the fruit of your womb, Jesus.*

———————

HEN he will pour forth words of wisdom . . . and give thanks to the Lord in prayer. The Lord will direct his counsel and his knowledge as he meditates upon the mysteries of God. —Sir 39:6

REFLECTION.   The Hail Mary said well is the force that puts the devil to flight.

It is the sanctification of the soul, the joy of Angels, the melody of the Elect, the canticle of the New Testament, the delight of Mary, and the glory of the Holy Trinity.

—*St. Louis Grignion de Montfort*

PRAYER.   *Holy Mary, Mother of God, pray for us sinners, now and at the hour of our death.*

OME time ago, God chose . . . that through my mouth the Gentiles would hear the word of the Gospel and believe. —Act 15:7

REFLECTION. By becoming the Mother of God, Mary was the means of the salvation of sinners.

In the same way, sinners are saved by proclaiming the praises of Mary. —St. Anselm

PRAYER. *O Mary, you are worthy of all praise. Let me praise you, speak to others about your merits, power, and mercy, and lead them to true devotion to you.*

 E imitators of me and observe those who conduct themselves after the pattern you have seen in us. —Phil 3:17

REFLECTION. Mary is a Model of all virtues who is more within our reach.

When we contemplate her, we do not feel overwhelmed by the splendor of the Divinity. On the contrary, we are attracted by the kinship of a common nature and strive more confidently to imitate her. —Pope Leo XIII

PRAYER. *O Mary, you are our Model in Christian Living. Help me to follow you at least to some degree in your great virtue and holiness, so that I may also follow you into heaven.*

REJOICE greatly in the Lord, and my soul is joyful in my God. For he has clothed me with a garment of salvation, and covered me with a robe of justice. —Isa 61:10

JULY 20

REFLECTION. Mary is living the perfect joy promised to the Church.

Her children on earth turn to her who is the Mother of Hope and Mother of Grace. They invoke her as the cause of our joy. —*Pope Paul VI*

PRAYER. *O Mary, you are the "Cause of Our Joy." Keep my eyes fixed on the eternal joys promised by your Divine Son, so that I will be filled with Christian joy all the days of my life.*

 URELY God is my savior; I will trust and be unafraid. My strength and my praise is the Lord, and he has become my salvation. —Isa 12:2

JULY 21

REFLECTION. Eve believed the devil—and the world perished!

Mary put her faith in the Angel of God—and the world was saved! —*St. Lawrence of Brindisi*

PRAYER. *O Mary, you are our refuge against evil. Teach me to put my faith in God when temptations assail me, so that I may deserve . to contribute to my salvation and reach my heavenly home.*

HOEVER would love life and see good days, . . . let him turn from evil and do good, seek peace and pursue it. —1 Pet 3:10-11

JULY 22

REFLECTION. True devotion to Mary is something holy.

It leads a soul to avoid sin and to imitate the virtues of Mary. —*St. Louis Grignion de Montfort*

PRAYER. *O Mary, genuine devotion to you helps us avoid sin and do good. Increase my devotion to you and make it influence every part of my life and every moment of my day.*

UT you . . . remain forever, and your name endures through all ages. . . . And the nations shall honor your name. —Ps 102 13-16

JULY 23

REFLECTION. The demons are ever anxious in their pursuit of souls.

However, they quickly abandon their prey at the sole Name of Mary. —*St. Bridget*

PRAYER. *O Mary, by God's Will your Name is a powerful remedy against sin and evil. Help me to invoke it in times of distress and praise it in times of joy.*

EMBER the days of your lowly estate. . . . Invoke the Lord and speak to the king on our behalf; save us from death. **JULY 24** —Est 4:8

REFLECTION. We are lost on a raging sea, far from God, and buffeted at every moment by storms.

We lie at the very jaws of spiritual death, and so we cry out: "Hail, Mary. . . ."

—*St. Anthony of Padua*

PRAYER. *O Mary, you are our beacon amid the dangers of this life. Enlighten my mind, open my heart, and curb my will, so that I may steer a safe course until I reach the eternal harbor.*

 WILL give you what you have not asked for. . . . And if you walk in my ways by obeying my statutes and commandments . . . , you will have a long life. **JULY 25** —1 Ki 3:13-14

REFLECTION. Mary has a great desire to be invoked by us so that she may dispense her favors to us in greater abundance.

So true is this that she is offended not only by those who speak ill of her but also by those who neglect to ask for her graces.

—*St. Bonaventure*

PRAYER. *O Mary, you are ready to pour down grace on us if we but ask for it. Help me to come to you in every need, so that I may receive your aid.*

HEN the Creator of all things gave me his command; he who created me decreed where I should dwell, saying, "Make your dwelling in Jacob, and in Israel receive your inheritance." —Sir 24:8

JULY 26

REFLECTION.   Christ remained in Mary's womb for nine months.

He will dwell in the tabernacle of the faith of the Church until the end of the world. And He will remain in the knowledge and love of the faithful for all eternity. —*St. Isaac of Stella*

PRAYER.   *O Mary, you were graced with God's presence both physically and spiritually. Obtain for me the grace to have Jesus dwelling in me forever.*

———————

HRIST loved the Church and delivered himself up for her to sanctify her, cleansing her in the bath of water by means of the word, so that he might present to himself the Church in all her majesty. —Eph 5:25-27

JULY 27

REFLECTION.   The Mother of God is a Model of the Church in the matter of faith, charity, and perfect union with God.

Through the gift and role of the Divine Motherhood, Mary is united with her Son and with the Church. —*Vatican II: The Church, 63*

PRAYER.   *O Mary, you are the Mother of the Church. Help me to be a loyal child of that Church, sharing in the Redemption of your Divine Son.*

A LL [the disciples] with one mind were united in constant prayer, together with the women, and Mary the Mother of Jesus, and his brethren.

JULY 28

—Act 1:14

REFLECTION. Mary was the perfect disciple of Christ, mirror of every virtue and embodiment of the evangelical beatitudes proclaimed by Jesus.

In her the whole Church attains the most authentic form of the perfect imitation of Christ.

—*Pope Paul VI*

PRAYER. *O Mary, you are the perfect follower of Jesus. Obtain for me the grace to follow you, so that I may be "another Christ" both in this world and in the next.*

Y OU who have no money, hurry, buy and eat. . . . Heed me, and eat what is good; your soul shall delight in rich fare.

JULY 29

—Isa 55:1-2

REFLECTION. O sinners, be not discouraged but have recourse to Mary in all your necessities.

Call her to your assistance, for you will always find her ready to help. It is God's will that she should help in every need. —*St. Basil*

PRAYER. *O Mary, you are the last hope of sinners. If I should have the misfortune to fall into serious sin, grant me the grace of true repentance.*

WALK in the path of justice, along the way of judgment, so that I may enrich those who love me and grant them abundant treasures. —Prov 8:20-21

REFLECTION. Mary's grace has given glory to heaven, a God to earth, and faith to the nations.

She has conferred death on vices, order on life, and a rule on morals. — *St. Peter Chrysologus*

PRAYER. *O Mary, obtain for me the grace to have you as my constant intercessor. In all difficulties let me call on your powerful aid, for you are God's beloved Daughter.*

 HE Gospel . . . is the power of God unto salvation to all who believe. . . . For in it is revealed the righteousness of God, from faith unto faith, as it is written, "The one who is just lives by faith." —Rom 1:16-17

REFLECTION. The Blessed Virgin will give you a share of her faith, a faith that will remove all concern with sensible and extraordinary things.

This faith will be living and animated by love so that you will act entirely out of love.

—*St. Louis Grignion de Montfort*

PRAYER. *O Mary, your great faith on earth has now become great vision in heaven. Make my faith strong so that I may live as a true follower of your Divine Son.*

HAT is man, that you magnify him, or pay him any attention? You examine him each day.

AUG. 1

—Job 7:17

REFLECTION. Heap together all the love of mothers for their children, all the love of husbands for their wives, and all the love of the Angels and Saints for their clients.

The total could never equal Mary's love for even a single soul! —*St. Alphonsus Liguori*

PRAYER. *O Mary, you have great love for souls. Let me return your love for me by loving others in you and your Divine Son—even those whom I find displeasing.*

 ECAUSE of his love and mercy he redeemed them and he lifted them up and carried them all the days of old.

AUG. 2

—Isa 63:9

REFLECTION. In her own life the Blessed Virgin lived an example of maternal love.

This love should animate all who cooperate in the apostolic mission of the Church for the regeneration of human beings.

—*Vatican II: Church, 65*

PRAYER. *O Mary, by your love you are a model for apostolic workers. Help me to carry out my Christian apostolate by praying for nonbelievers and bearing witness to your Divine Son for them.*

HE is unique, my dove, my perfect one, her mother's chosen, the favorite of her parent. . . . The daughters saw her and . . . declared her most blessed.

AUG. 3

—SS 6:9

REFLECTION. The look of Mary, the smile of Mary, the sweetness of Mary, the majesty of Mary, Queen of heaven and earth!

Mary's beauty stands out among all other beauties, which pale next to hers. Mary is the most beautiful of God's creatures.

—*Pope Pius X11*

PRAYER. *O Mary, you are all-beautiful and worthy of praise. Help me to render you the honor you deserve by following your inspirations and imitating your shining example.*

DO not be conformed to this world, but be transformed by renewing your mind that you may discern what is the good and pleasing and perfect will of God.

AUG. 4

—Rom 12:2

REFLECTION. Do you know the surest way to learn the will of God?

It is the way of prayer to our good Mother Mary!

—*St. John Vianney*

PRAYER. *O Mary, you are the revealer of God's will to us. Help me to know what God's will is for me in every situation and to carry out that will with diligence and love.*

EVEN if I am made the libation for the sacrificial service of your faith, I am glad and rejoice with all of you.

AUG. 5

—Phil 2:17

REFLECTION. The Immaculate Conception also entails sacrifice on the part of Mary.

Therefore, we cannot consider ourselves favored children of the Lord and His Mother if our lives know nothing of sacrifice.

—*Pope John XXIII*

PRAYER. *O Mary, you shared the sacrifices of Jesus from the privations at His Birth, to the renunciations of the Hidden Life, to the martyrdom on Calvary. Join my little daily sacrifices to His.*

AS the soldiers listened to what she had to say, they gazed upon her face and marveled at her beauty.

AUG. 6

—Jud 10:14

REFLECTION. The thought and the countenance of Mary inspire the purity of life that is the first dignity of human beings.

They also constitute the salvation of those who struggle against evil and those who are called to greater perfection of life. —*Pope Pius XI*

PRAYER. *O Mary, the thought of you leads to salvation. Let me meditate on your spiritual beauty, so that I too may be saved.*

D O not labor for the food that perishes but for that which endures for eternal life, which the Son of Man will give you. —Jn 6:27

AUG. 7

REFLECTION.   Ask the Virgin Mary constantly to come to you with her glorious Son. Be bold.

Ask her to give you her Son, Who in the Blessed Sacrament is truly the Food of your soul. She will give Him to you readily.

—St. Cajetan

PRAYER.   *O Mary, you are ever ready to give us the Food of our souls. Help me prepare through prayer and good works for the visit of the great King, Who is Christ your Son.*

P ETER answered him, "Lord, to whom shall we go? You have the words of eternal life. We have come to believe and to know that you are the Christ, the Son of God." —Jn 6:68-69

AUG. 8

REFLECTION.   O Mary, to whom else shall we go? You have the words of eternal life!

These are the prayers by which you intervene on our behalf before God. Indeed, you never cease to work wonders for us.

—St. Germanus

PRAYER.   *O Mary, like the words of Jesus, your prayerful words on our behalf bring salvation. Never cease to pray for me "till in heaven eternally your love and bliss I share."*

T HE Lord has bared his holy arm in the sight of the Gentiles; all the ends of the earth shall see the salvation of our God. —Isa 52:10

AUG. 9

REFLECTION. Through this Virgin, the whole earth is filled with the glory of God.

Through this Virgin, all have known the great God. All have seen the salvation of God.

—*St. Ildephonsus*

PRAYER. *O Mary, through you, salvation came to the world. May those peoples who are still without the knowledge of your Divine Son come to know, love, and serve Him.*

———————

B LESSED is the soul that fears the Lord. . . . The eyes of the Lord watch over those who love him; he is their mighty shield and strong support.

—Sir 34:15-16

AUG. 10

REFLECTION. O Mary, Mother of Love, love your Jesus and mine for me.

And make me share the love that you bear for Him! —*St. John Eudes*

PRAYER. *O Mary, your love for your Divine Son was greater than the combined love of all other humans. Increase my love for Jesus and let it be expressed in actions.*

117

THE Lord is far from the wicked, but he will hear the prayers of the just.
—Prov 15:29

AUG. 11

REFLECTION. Mary's prayers and requests are so powerful with God that they pass for commands with His Majesty.

He never resists the prayer of His dear Mother because it is always humble and in accord with His will. —*St. Louis Grignion de Montfort*

PRAYER. *O Mary, your prayers for us are always conformed to the will of God. Help me to conform my will and my prayers to the will of your Divine Son, Jesus.*

I GO to prepare a place for you. . . . And I will come back and take you to be with me, so that where I am, there you will be.
—Jn 14:2-3

AUG. 12

REFLECTION. O Mary, you who are the Mother of Life had to remain always with Life.

For you, death could never be anything more than sleep and the Assumption anything more than an act of waking up. —*St. Germanus*

PRAYER. *O Mary, your glory of the Assumption is a pledge of our glory. Help me to live in such a way that when Jesus returns for me He will find me worthy to join you in heaven.*

ET the faithful rejoice in glory; let them sing for joy in their beds. Let the praises of God be in their mouths.

AUG. 13

—Ps 149:5-6

REFLECTION.   O Mary, may all nations glorify your Immaculate Heart!

May the whole earth invoke and bless your Immaculate Heart!   *—St. John Vianney*

PRAYER.   *O Mary, our human speech is too feeble to honor you as we ought. Grant that I may never cease praising you and invoking your Immaculate Heart.*

O the people stood far off and said to Moses, "You speak to us, and we will hear. But do not let God speak to us, or we shall die."

AUG. 14

—Ex 20:18-19

REFLECTION.   If you want to grow in perfection, you cannot advance by yourselves—you need a guide.

Hence, when you go to God, go through Mary and with Mary!   *—St. Maximilian Kolbe*

PRAYER.   *O Mary, you are our Mediatrix with the God of all. Help me to grow in grace and holiness, so that I may one day reach your Divine Son in the bliss of heaven.*

THOSE who sow in tears shall reap rejoicing. They go forth weeping, carrying the seed to be sown. They come back rejoicing, carrying their sheaves.
—Ps 126:5-6

REFLECTION. Mary sowed much in tears while on earth, and now she is reaping much in heavenly joy.

The same will be true for us. The more spiritual victories we obtain while on earth, the more we will receive in heaven. —*St. Bernard*

PRAYER. *O Mary, grant me the grace to obtain daily spiritual victories over myself, the world, and the devil. Let me imitate your faithfulness and so share your glory.*

FROM ivory palaces the music of stringed instruments brings you joy . . . ; the queen stands at your right hand in gold of Ophir. —Ps 45:9-10

REFLECTION. The heavenly host came forth rejoicing in festal array, to meet the Mother of God.

Surrounded with effulgent light, Mary was led amid praises and canticles to the throne prepared for her from the world's beginning.
—*St. Jerome*

PRAYER. *O Mary, at the Assumption you were solemnly taken into the glory of heaven. Fix my eyes on that glory, so that I may put up with the adversities of this world.*

FORGIVE the sins of this people according to your great mercy, as you have been merciful to them . . . until now.

AUG.
17

—Num 14:19

REFLECTION. When we pray to the Mother of God, we are heard more quickly than when we call directly on Jesus—for He is not only our Lord but also our Judge.

However, Mary has no other office except to show compassion. —*St. Anselm*

PRAYER. *O Mary, help me to imitate you and your Divine Son by showing kindness to others when they hurt me.*

———————

 IT is I who girded you . . . , so that from the rising of the sun to the west where it sets, men may know that there is none besides me.

AUG.
18

—Isa 45:5-6

REFLECTION. O Blessed Virgin, nothing resists your power. God the Father looks upon your glory as if it were His own.

And God the Son takes delight in glorifying you and grants your every petition as if He were paying a debt. —*St. Gregory of Nicomedia*

PRAYER. *O Mary you have the ear of God. Beg Him to have mercy on us and to send peace to a tormented world.*

YOU come forth to deliver your people. . . . You make a way in the sea with your horses amid the churning of many waters. **AUG. 19** —Hab 3:13-15

REFLECTION. The Heart of Mary is a sun that spreads its rays and its warmth throughout the world.

It is constantly working in every possible way for the salvation of souls. —*St. John Eudes*

PRAYER. *O Immaculate Heart of Mary, be my salvation! I put all my trust in you for time and for eternity.*

 ALL should honor the Son even as they honor the Father. Whoever does not honor the Son does not honor the Father who sent him. **AUG. 20** —Jn 5:23

REFLECTION. Let us not imagine that we obscure the glory of the Son by the great praise we lavish on His Mother.

The more Mary is honored, the greater is the glory of her Son. —*St. Bernard*

PRAYER. *O Mary, the more we honor you, the more we honor Jesus. And the more we honor Jesus, the more we honor the Father. Let me heap praises on you all the day long.*

HEN Jesus had brought about man's purgation from sins, he took his seat at the right hand of the Majesty in heaven. —Heb 1:3

AUG. 21

REFLECTION. Mary sits at the right hand of Jesus like a Queen.

She is the most safe refuge for and the most fruitful helper of all who are in danger, so there is no reason to fear. —*St. Pius X*

PRAYER. *O Mary, you are the Mediatrix of All Grace. Keep me under your guidance, your care, your benevolence, and your protection, so that I will have no reason to despair.*

 OUR renown spread forth among the nations for your beauty, which was perfect since I placed my splendor upon you. —Ezek 16:14

AUG. 22

REFLECTION. Mary consented to be the Mother of the Eternal Word.

At that very moment, she merited to be made the Queen of the world and all creatures.

—*St. Alphonsus Liguori*

PRAYER. *O Mary, you are our Queen. Reign over all hearts by the queenly power of your love, so that the Kingdom of your Divine Son may come upon earth.*

THE lowly may be pardoned through mercy, but the mighty will be tested with rigor.

AUG.
23

—Wis 6:6

REFLECTION. When the Blessed Virgin conceived the Eternal Word in her womb and gave Him birth, she obtained half the Kingdom of God.

She became Queen of Mercy, and her Son remained King of Justice! —*St. Thomas Aquinas*

PRAYER. *O Mary, you are the Queen and Exemplar of Mercy. In imitation of you, let me be humble and merciful toward others, so that I too may receive mercy and pardon.*

THIS saying is true and worthy of full acceptance: Christ Jesus came into the world to save sinners. Of these I am the worst.

AUG.
24

—1 Tim 1:15

REFLECTION. As the Queen of Mercy, Mary throws open the abyss of God's mercies to anyone she pleases, when she pleases, and as she pleases.

Hence, there are no sinners who will be lost when she intercedes for them! —*St. Bernard*

PRAYER. *O Mary, you dispense the merits of Christ's Redemption to all sinners. Pour down on me the Divine Mercy, so that I may repent for my past sins and strive to avoid sin in the future.*

ET your heart receive my words. Keep my commands, and you shall live! Get wisdom, get prudence.

AUG. 25

—Prov 4:4-5

REFLECTION.   Praise be to Mary!

Let all hearts give themselves to Mary so that she may fill them with her Heart and the Heart of Jesus!

—*St. John Eudes*

PRAYER.   *O Mary, you are the Queen of Hearts! Mold my heart after your own, so that it may possess the sentiments of true Christian living and reflect the Heart of your Divine Son.*

———————

EHOLD, as the eyes of servants are on their master's hands, . . . so are our eyes raised to the Lord, our God, till he have mercy on us.

AUG. 26

—Ps 123:2

REFLECTION.   I want to be a devoted servant of the Heavenly Father.

Therefore, I faithfully desire to be the servant of the Mother.

—*St. Ildephonsus*

PRAYER.   *O Mary, let me be completely devoted to you. Only in this way can I be a true servant of the Heavenly Father and of your Divine Son Jesus.*

Y heart overflows with a noble theme; as I recite my poem to the king, my tongue is the pen of a swift scribe. **AUG. 27** —Ps 45:2

REFLECTION. The glorious Virgin was raised to the dignity of Mother of the King of kings.

Accordingly, the Church honors her with the radiant title of Queen and asks us to do the same. —*St. Alphonsus Liguori*

PRAYER. *O Mary, you are the Queen of the Universe. Grant that I may praise you as you deserve and reap the spiritual benefits of life-long dedication to your service.*

 E is not far from each of us. For "In him we live and move and have our being," as some of your own poets have said. **AUG. 28** —Act 17:27-28

REFLECTION. I hold that Mary is now with Christ and in Christ.

She is in Christ, because "in Him we live and move and have our being." She is with Christ, because she has been assumed into glory.

—*St. Augustine*

PRAYER. *O Mary, you live in glory with your Divine Son. Let me remain united with you and live and move in God while on earth, so that I may be with Him in the glory of heaven.*

TRENUOUS labor is the lot of all human beings . . . from the day when they emerge from their mother's womb until the day when they return to the mother of us all.

AUG. 29

—Sir 40:1

REFLECTION.   Mary is a Queen because she is a Mother, the Immaculate Mother of God, a completely Divine Mother.

She is thus the Queen of heaven and earth, of Angels and human beings.

—*St. Maximilian Kolbe*

PRAYER.   *O Mary, you are the Mother of all the living and Queen of all. Watch over me by your motherly care. And intercede with the King of kings on my behalf.*

───────────

OD made two great lights: a greater one to rule the day, and a lesser one to rule the night.

AUG. 30

—Gen 1:16

REFLECTION.   The moon, standing between the sun and the earth, transmits to the earth whatever light it receives from the sun.

In like manner, Mary stands between God and human beings and pours His grace upon us.   —*St. Bonaventure*

PRAYER.   *O Mary, you flood us with Christ's supernatural brightness. Grant me the graces to flee the proximate occasions of sin and remain true to my Christian vocation.*

YE has not seen nor has ear heard, neither has it entered the human heart . . . what God has prepared for those who love him. —1 Cor 2:9

AUG. 31

REFLECTION. Eye has not seen, ear has not heard, and the human heart has not felt what God has prepared for those who love Him.

Who, then, can dare speak about what God has prepared for His Mother! —*St. Bernard*

PRAYER. *O Mary, you are now enjoying the ineffable reward prepared for you. Let me dwell often on the joys that await me if I remain faithful to God's will for me.*

Y just one is near, my savior has gone forth . . . ; the coastlands look for me and wait patiently for my arm. —Isa 51:5

SEPT. 1

REFLECTION. Because Jesus redeemed us, He is our Lord and our King.

In the same way, the Blessed Virgin is our Lady and our Queen on account of the unique manner in which she assisted in the Redemption, offering her Son to the Father for the salvation of the world. —*Pope Pius XII*

PRAYER. *O Mary, most noble Queen of the world, plead for peace and salvation in our behalf, for you have brought forth Christ the Lord, the Savior of us all.*

JUST as the living Father has sent me and I live because of the Father, so also the one who feeds on me will live because of me. —Jn 6:57

REFLECTION.   Every grace granted to human beings has three degrees in order.

From God it is communicated to Christ; from Christ it passes to the Blessed Virgin; and from the Blessed Virgin it comes to us.

—*St. Bernardine of Siena*

PRAYER.   *O Mary, you are the Channel of Divine Grace for us. Grant that I may be receptive to every grace earmarked for me and may cooperate with it to the full.*

EPHRAIM is my favored son; he is a tender child. . . . I still remember him. My heart stirs for him, and I will surely show him compassion.   —Jer 31:20

REFLECTION.   Mary far surpasses all other mothers in glory and holiness as well as in kindness and sweetness.

Come before her with a contrite and humbled heart. You will find her more prompt and more tender in loving you than all other mothers.

—*St. Gregory*

PRAYER.   *"O Mother of the Word Incarnate, to you do I come, before you I stand, sinful and sorrowful. Despise not my petitions, but in your mercy hear and answer me."*

T HE kingdom of heaven is like a treasure hidden in a field. When a person
finds it he hides it again; then, filled
with joy, he goes and sells all that he
has and buys that field.   —Mt 13:44

REFLECTION.   Every good, every help, and
every grace that human beings have received
and will receive from God until the end of time
came and will come to them by the intercession
and through the hands of Mary.

When we find Mary, we find all!

—Blessed Raymond Jordano

PRAYER.   *O Mary, you are the "treasure hidden
in a field." Let me be willing to give up all
things so that I may never be separated from
you and your Divine Son.*

W AIT yet a little and I will show
you. I still have some things to
say in God's behalf.   —Job 36:2

REFLECTION.   Mary is the echo of God. If we
say "Mary," she will answer "God."

That is why union with her is always followed by union with God.

—St. Louis Grignion de Montfort

PRAYER.   *O Mary, you are the Echo of God. Let
me imitate you in echoing the teaching of Jesus
to others both in my words and in my deeds.*

THE Lord does not delay in his promises, but is patient for your sake, not wanting anyone to perish, but all to turn to repentance.

SEPT. 6

—2 Pet 3:9

REFLECTION. Mary does not know how to refuse compassion. She has never learned how to let the comfortless go away uncomforted.

And so, she will persuade her Son to pardon me. —*St. Bonaventure*

PRAYER. *O Mary, you are the Mother of Compassion. Help me to show compassion to others, so that I may benefit from your compassion and that of your Divine Son.*

WHEN the Lord has brought you into the . . . land that flows with milk and honey, you shall celebrate this sacred rite in this month.

SEPT. 7

—Ex 13:5

REFLECTION. Mary is a land that, though it has never been sown, brings forth fruit that gives food to all creatures.

She is a land on which rest the blessings of the Lord. —*St. Theodore the Studite*

PRAYER. *O Mary, you are the "land that flows with milk and honey." Fill me with the blessings that flow from such a Divine land, so that I too may bring forth fruits worthy of salvation.*

SHOOT shall spring up from the stump of Jesse, and out of his roots a flower shall blossom. The Spirit of the Lord shall rest upon him.

SEPT.
8

—Isa 11:1-2

REFLECTION.   The birth of the Mother of God is the prelude to the union of the Word with flesh.

Today the Virgin is born, tended and formed, and prepared for her role as Mother of God, Who is the Universal King of the ages.

—*St. Andrew of Crete*

PRAYER.   *O Mary, the birth of Jesus from you was the dawn of our salvation. May the celebration of your birthday bring the world closer to lasting peace and redound to my salvation.*

———————

 E gave some as apostles . . . , for strengthening the body of Christ, until we all attain to the unity of the faith and of the knowledge of the Son of God, to perfect manhood.

SEPT.
9

—Eph 4:11-13

REFLECTION.   Mary meditated on all she had come to know through reading, listening, and observing.

She grew in faith, increased in merits, and was more consumed by the fire of charity.

—*St. Lawrence Justinian*

PRAYER.   *O Mary, you grew spiritually through meditation. Help me to set aside some time— no matter how little—for meditation each day, so that I may grow to the full stature of Christ.*

LORD, you searched me and you know me; you know when I sit and when I stand. You discern my thoughts from afar. —Ps 139:1-2

SEPT. 10

REFLECTION. What joy it is for us to dwell on the fact that Mary is our Mother!

Why should we fear? She loves us and knows our weakness! —*St. Theresa of Lisieux*

PRAYER. *O Mary, you love us and watch over us. Let me never forget that you are a true Mother to me—always ready to lead me to your Divine Son.*

WILL give you a different heart and put a new spirit within you, taking from you your heart of stone and giving you a heart of flesh. I will put my spirit within you. —Ezek 36:26-27

SEPT. 11

REFLECTION. When devotion to Mary begins in anyone, it produces the same effect that our Lady's birth produces in the world.

It ends the night of sin and leads a person along the bright path of virtue.

—*St. Alphonsus Liguori*

PRAYER. *O Mary, great are the benefits of devotion to you. Help me to be more devoted to you—through prayer, meditation, and good works. Give me a Marian spirit.*

HE Father. . . will give you another Advocate to be with you forever, the Spirit of truth. . . . He will dwell with you and be in you. —Jn 14:16-17

SEPT. 12

REFLECTION.   In the Church our souls are espoused to the Holy Spirit.

It is Mary whose prayer wins strength, joy, and consolation for us. And it is Mary who gives joy to the Divine Bridegroom by inspiring our wills with love for Him.

—*Venerable Francis Libermann*

PRAYER.   *O Mary, help me to be united with the Holy Spirit. Teach me to follow the holy inspirations and loving guidance of this Divine Guest of my soul*

F the Son [he says]: "Your throne, O God, will stand forever and ever; and righteousness will be the scepter of your kingdom." —Heb 1:8

SEPT. 13

REFLECTION.   I salute you, O Mother Mary!

You are the throne of God as well as the honor, the glory, and the strength of our Church! —*St. John Chrysostom*

PRAYER.   *O Mary, you were like a throne for your Divine Son. Teach me to enthrone Jesus in my heart and to render constant homage to Him by my words and my actions.*

GOD forbid that I should boast save in the cross of our Lord Jesus Christ, through whom the world is crucified to me, and I to the world. —Gal 6:14

REFLECTION. The Cross is the School of Love. Let us remember that Love lives on and is nourished by sacrifices.

Let us always have recourse to the Immaculate Mother to preserve our peace of mind.

—*St. Maximilian Kolbe*

PRAYER. *O Mary, you followed Jesus by carrying your cross. Help me to bear the crosses and trials that come my way each day. Let them never separate me from you or your Divine Son.*

SIMEON said to Mary, "Behold, this child is destined for the fall and rise of many in Israel, and for a sign that will be contradicted. And your own soul a sword will pierce." —Lk 2:34-35

REFLECTION. On Calvary the sufferings of Mary most holy reached their height.

Mary's presence at the foot of the Cross constituted a most special participation in the Redemptive Death of her Son. —*Pope John Paul II*

PRAYER. *"Virgin of all virgins blest!/hasten to my fond request:/let me share your grief Divine./Let me, to my latest breath,/in my body bear the death,/of your dying Son Divine."*

I BROUGHT up children and honored them, but they have disowned me! An ox knows its master, and an ass, its owner's manger; but . . . my people have not understood.

SEPT. 16

—Isa 1:2-3

REFLECTION. Women who seek involvement in community affairs should look to Mary.

Taken into dialogue with God, Mary gives her active and responsible consent. . . to the event of world importance known as the Incarnation of the Word. —*Pope Paul VI*

PRAYER. *O Mary, your decision affected the world's salvation. Teach me how to take part in decisions that affect world, Church, and community as well as my own salvation.*

AS the body is one though it has many members, and all the members of the body, though many, are one body, so it is also with Christ. For in the same Spirit we were all baptized into one body.

SEPT. 17

—1 Cor 12:12-13

REFLECTION. All favors, graces, and heavenly inspirations come from Christ as from the Head.

All then descend to the body through Mary, since—just as in the human body—it is by the neck that the Head gives life to the limbs.

—*St. Robert Bellarmine*

PRAYER. *O Mary, you are the Mother of the Mystical Body. Enable me to act as a true member of that Body—ever ready to render loving assistance to all other members.*

NOW you are light in the Lord. Walk as children of light, for light produces all goodness and justice and truth. —Eph 5:8-9

SEPT.
18

REFLECTION. For those who believe in our Lord Jesus Christ, for those who believe in the Church, behold the Mother: Mary!

Therefore, everything in the life of Christians is given light by this sweetest of notes: Mary our Mother! —*Pope John XXIII*

PRAYER. *O Mary, you give light to everything in our lives. Enlighten my mind and open my heart, so that I may learn and carry out the things that are pleasing to your Divine Son.*

SHE opens her mouth to wisdom, and on her tongue is the law of mercy. . . . Her children rise up and call her blessed. —Prov 31:26-28

SEPT.
19

REFLECTION. When we who are devoted to Mary call her Mother, we are not using empty words or just speaking at random.

She is our Mother—not by the flesh, of course, but spiritually; the Mother of our souls, of our salvation. —*St. Alphonsus Liguori*

PRAYER. *O Mary, I thank you for consenting to become the Mother of our souls. Grant me the grace to love you and your Divine Son as you deserve.*

THIS is the gate of the Lord, the just shall enter by it. I will give thanks to you, for you have heard my plea and have become my Savior. —Ps 118:20-21

REFLECTION.   How can Mary be otherwise than full of grace?

She has been made the Ladder to Paradise, the Gate of Heaven, and the most true Mediatrix between God and human beings.

—*St. Lawrence Justinian*

PRAYER.   *O Mary, you are the Gate of Heaven. Help me to live as a true child of yours, so that upon my death I may deserve to enter heaven through you.*

———————

GOD sent the spirit of his Son into our hearts, crying out, "Abba, Father!" So you are no longer a servant but a son, and if a son then also an heir, through God. —Gal 4:6-7

REFLECTION.   Mary has conceived the Divine Word.

She has thus become the heaven that enclosed the Divinity in her womb for the purpose of exalting mortals to the great dignity of kinship with God. —*St. Ephrem*

PRAYER.   *O Mary, you were the Associate of Jesus in His work of making us children of God. Help me to prize this Divine adoption above all things and ever seek to live as a true child of God.*

THEN the king asked, "What is it, Queen Esther? What is your request? Even up to half the kingdom, it will be given you."

—Est 5:3

REFLECTION. Imagine that all the stars were tongues and all the grains of sand were words.

They would still fall short of recounting all the glories bestowed by God on Mary's soul.

—*St. Thomas of Villanova*

PRAYER. *O Mary, you have received untold blessings from God. Help me to speak of your glories to others and bear witness to your intercessory power with your Divine Son.*

FOR so the Lord has commanded . . . , "I have set you as a light to the Gentiles, that you may be a means of salvation to all the world."

—Act 13:47

REFLECTION. We find ourselves on earth as in a tempestuous sea, a desert, and a vale of tears.

But Mary is the Star of the Sea, the Solace of our desert, and the Light that guides us to heaven.

—*St. John Bosco*

PRAYER. *O Mary, you are our unfailing Guide to heaven. Make me desire holiness, and lead me along the right paths, so that at journey's end I may deserve to be with you and Jesus.*

L OVE is patient and kind. . . . It bears with all things, believes all things, hopes all things, endures all things.

SEPT.
24

—1 Cor 13:4-7

REFLECTION.   Do not be surprised that Mary is said to be a martyr in spirit.

According to Paul, one of the greatest crimes of the Gentiles was lack of love. This was far from the Heart of Mary. Let it be far from her servants as well.   —St. Bernard

PRAYER.   *O Mary, you are the Mother of Fair Love. Fill my heart with Divine love, so that I may never lack for love and may learn to offer my life as a gift of love to Jesus.*

———————

Y OU imitated us and the Lord, receiving the word . . . with joy given by the Holy Spirit, so that you became a pattern to all the believers.

SEPT.
25

—1 Thes 1:6-7

REFLECTION.   Christ is the only way to the Father and the ultimate Model to be imitated.

But devotion to the Blessed Virgin, subordinated to worship of the Divine Savior and in connection with it, also has a great pastoral effectiveness and constitutes a force for renewing Christian living.   —Pope Paul V!

PRAYER.   *O Mary, grant me a genuine devotion to you. May it help me to imitate your Divine Son on earth, so that I may be with Him forever in heaven.*

AKE disciples of every nation . . . , teaching them to obey all that I have commanded you. And behold, I am with you all days, even to the end of the world. —Mt 28:19-20

REFLECTION. Those who belong to Mary should do all they can to win the hearts of others to her.

And Mary will enlighten those hearts, enkindle them with the love of her Maternal Heart, and inflame them with the fire of charity that burns in the Divine Heart of Jesus.

—*St. Maximilian Kolbe*

PRAYER. *O Mary, you are the Queen of the Missions. Help me to offer my prayers and good works to gain disciples for you, so that you can lead them to Jesus.*

ISE up, you ancient portals, that the king of glory may enter in! Who is this king of glory? The Lord of power and might. —Ps 24:7-8

REFLECTION. Since the flesh of Mary was no different from that of Jesus, how can we deny to the Mother the same royal dignity we find in the Son?

The glory of the Son is not something shared with His Mother, but her glory too!

—*St. Arnold the Abbot*

PRAYER. *O Mary, you are the Queen of Glory! Teach me to be your devoted servant, serving Jesus the King as well.*

AMEN, amen, I say to you, whoever welcomes anyone I send welcomes me, and whoever welcomes me welcomes him who sent me. —Jn 13:20

REFLECTION. To go to Jesus through Mary is truly to honor Jesus Christ.

It indicates that we do not esteem ourselves worthy of approaching His infinite holiness directly, that we need Mary to be our Mediatrix with Him, our Mediator.

—*St. Louis Grignion de Montfort*

PRAYER. *O Mary, you are our Mediatrix with Jesus and with the Father. Plead for us now, as once you shared with us the pains, fears, and sorrows of life on earth.*

COME out from them and stay apart, says the Lord, . . . and I will be a father to you, and you shall be my sons and daughters.

—2 Cor 6:17-18

REFLECTION. If Jesus is the Father, Mary is the Mother of our souls. She gave us Jesus and supernatural life.

She offered her Son on Calvary for our redemption and gave us birth in the life of grace.

—*St. Alphonsus Liguori*

PRAYER. *O Mother of my soul, take care of it. Help me to keep it continually united with you, free from all sin, and immersed in the state of grace.*

O other woman from one end of the earth to the other is her equal in beauty and in wisdom of speech!

—Jud 11:21

REFLECTION. Look closely at the Blessed Virgin Mary.

There is nothing of virtue, nothing of beauty, nothing of splendor or glory that does not shine in her. —*St. Jerome*

PRAYER. *O Mary, you are the Fountain of Beauty and Model of Virtue. Help me to imitate your humility, which crowns all your other virtues.*

EAR the sound of my prayer, when I cry to you, lifting up my hands toward your holy sanctuary. —Ps 28:2

REFLECTION. The Blessed Virgin never shall fail to protect me when I call upon her.

When I am troubled, I quickly turn to her. And like the most tender of mothers she looks after me. —*St. Theresa of Lisieux*

PRAYER. *O Mary, you are the Protector of your people. In times of affliction, let me always turn to you with the confident assurance that you will come to my aid.*

THE Ancient of Days took his seat. . . .
Thousands upon thousands attended
to him, and ten thousand times ten
thousand stood before him.

OCT.
2

—Dan 7:9-10

REFLECTION. This very honorable Virgin is an abyss of virtues.

She precedes the Seraphim and is over the Cherubim! —*St. John Damascene*

PRAYER. *O Mary, you are the Queen of Angels. Grant me the grace to be truly devoted to the Angels, especially my Guardian Angel, and to follow all the inspirations they bring me from your Divine Son.*

STEEM her, and she will honor you; she
will bring you glory if you embrace her
. . . ; a noble crown will she present to
you.

OCT.
3

—Prov 4:8-9

REFLECTION. Experience has shown that to inculcate love for the Mother of God deeply in souls there is nothing more efficacious than the practice of the Rosary.

We exhort all the faithful to practice this devotion. —*Pope Leo XIII*

PRAYER. *O Mary, you are the Queen of the Holy Rosary. Let me say my Rosary faithfully and so grow in love for you and Jesus.*

WILL make known your name, for you have been my protector and my support. You have rescued me from destruction.

OCT. 4

—Sir 51:1-2

REFLECTION. When we speak the Name of Mary, heaven becomes more beautiful and earth rejoices.

The demons are terrified and vanish like dust in the wind. —*St. Francis of Assisi*

PRAYER. *O Mary, your holy Name is a never-failing treasure. May it be always on my lips and in my heart—in times of distress and in times of happiness.*

 EFLECT on what I am telling you, for the Lord will give you understanding in all things.

OCT. 5

—2 Tim 2:7

REFLECTION. Happy are those who recite the . Holy Rosary with understanding.

They will learn all that is of faith, light, hope, and love in it. —*St. Clement Hofbauer*

PRAYER. *O Mary, your Rosary is a School of the Faith. Let me recite it with understanding, so that I may grow in faith, light, hope, and love.*

FILLED with the Holy Spirit, Elizabeth cried out . . . , "Blessed are you among women, and blessed is the fruit of your womb."

OCT.

6

—Lk 1:41-42

REFLECTION. Jesus, Son of Mary, has no likeness among men, nor has Mary any likeness among women.

He is the most beautiful of the living. She is a splendid dawn rising. —*St. Bruno*

PRAYER. *O Mary, you are blessed among women. May all women take you as a Model of Womanhood and thus obtain greater blessings for the world from your Divine Son.*

BUT thanks be to God who always leads us in victory in Christ Jesus and manifests through us the fragrance of the knowledge of him everywhere.

OCT.

7

—2 Cor 2:14

REFLECTION. The Rosary represents a symbol of Mary's graces.

Christians invoke her as "Queen of the Most Holy Rosary," which conjures up the brilliant conquests of faith over evil and over religious ignorance. —*Pope Pius XII*

PRAYER. *O Mary, you are Our Lady of the Rosary. Enable me to share in the spiritual victories over evil that you accomplish with Jesus' help through the Rosary.*

THOSE whom he foreknew he also predestined to be formed in the likeness of his Son, so that he might be the firstborn of many brothers.

—Rom 8:29

REFLECTION. The Rosary in particular is a sign of predestination.

Our fidelity in reciting it is a sure sign of salvation. —*Blessed Alain de la Roche*

PRAYER. *O Mary, your Rosary is a sign of salvation. Help me and all who recite it to advance rapidly in grace, live perfectly, die peacefully, and rise surely to eternal life.*

INSTRUCT me in the way of your precepts, and I will meditate on your marvelous works. —Ps 119:27

REFLECTION. The Rosary calls for a quiet rhythm and a lingering pace, helping the individual to meditate on the Mysteries of the Lord's life as seen through the eyes of Mary.

Thus, the unfathomable riches of these Mysteries are unfolded. —*Pope Paul VI*

PRAYER. *O Mary, when I say the Rosary, I meditate on Christ's Mysteries in union with you. Help me to imitate what they contain and obtain what they promise.*

HE life that I now live in the body, I live by faith in the Son of God who loved me and gave himself up for me.

OCT. 10

—Gal 2:20

REFLECTION. How could love not be made more fervent by the Rosary? We meditate on the Suffering and Death of our Redeemer and the Sorrows of His afflicted Mother.

Will we not make a return for the love received?

—*Pope Pius XI*

PRAYER. *O Mary, what return can I make to your Divine Son and to you for all that you have done for me? I offer you all that I am and all that I have—wrapped up in my daily Rosary.*

Y soul longs for your salvation; I trust in your word. My eyes fail longing for your promise.

OCT. 11

—Ps 119:81-82

REFLECTION. The well-meditated Rosary consists in a threefold element.

For each decade there is a picture, and for each picture a threefold emphasis, which is simultaneously: mystical contemplation, intimate reflection, and pious intention.

—*Pope John XXIII*

PRAYER. *O Mary, teach me to understand each Mystery by contemplation, apply it to my life by reflection, and offer it for some personal or public good by intention.*

NOW hope that is not really hope. . . . But if we hope for what we do not yet see, we wait with patience.

—Rom 8:24-25

OCT.
12

REFLECTION.   The Rosary enlivens the hope for things above that endure forever.

As we meditate on the glory of Jesus and His Mother, we see heaven opened and are heartened in our striving to gain the eternal home.

—Pope Pius XI

PRAYER.   *O Mary, as I recite my Rosary, foster the virtue of hope in me. Teach me to wait with patience for the fulfillment of God's promises.*

BE persevering in prayer; be watchful and thankful. At the same time, pray for us also.

—Col 4:2-3

OCT.
13

REFLECTION.   Rising or going to bed, leaving or returning, away or at home, I have the "Hail Mary" always on my lips. I am insuperable when I say it.

To become perfect, say a Rosary a day.

—St. Louis Grignion de Montfort

PRAYER.   *O Mary, let me follow St. Louis' advice and say a Rosary a day. But if I cannot always do that, let me at least say a "Hail Mary" in your honor.*

NE who sows in the spirit will reap everlasting life from the spirit. Let us not grow weary in doing good.

—Gal 6:8

OCT. 14

REFLECTION. The Rosary is all-powerful to touch the Heart of our Lady.

It is the most excellent and fruitful type of prayer for obtaining above all eternal life.

—Pope Leo XIII

PRAYER. *O Mary, help me to recite my Rosary faithfully. Grant that it may keep me close to you on earth and gain for me eternal life and union with you in heaven.*

 HERE were certain Greeks among those who had gone up to worship on the feast.... They came to Philip ... and asked him, "Sir, we wish to see Jesus."

—Jn 12:20-21

OCT. 15

REFLECTION. The Rosary is a devotion that, through the Blessed Mother, leads us to Jesus.

It is He Who is the goal of this long and repeated invocation to Mary.

—Pope Paul VI

PRAYER. *O Mary, the Rosary is our ticket to Jesus. We speak to you and we come to Jesus. Help me to recite my Rosary with attention and devotion.*

N that day, you will know that I am in my Father, and you in me and I in you. —Jn 14:20

OCT. 16

REFLECTION. O Mary, our sweet hope, make us experience your power with the loving Heart of Jesus.

Employ your credit to make us lodge there forever. —*St. Margaret Mary Alacoque*

PRAYER. *O Mary, you are the Mother of Hope. I put all my trust in you. Keep me safe in the Heart of your Divine Son forever.*

———————

HE manifestation of the Spirit is given to all for some benefit. . . . All these things are produced by the same Spirit who distributes to everyone as he wills. —1 Cor 12:7-11

OCT. 17

REFLECTION. The Holy Spirit distributes His gifts, His virtues, and His grace through Mary.

He distributes them to whomever He wills, as many as He wills, and the way He wills.

—*St. Ignatius of Antioch*

PRAYER. *O Mary, it is through you that the Spirit pours forth His graces. Help me to cooperate fully with the particular gifts of the Spirit that are bestowed on me.*

ASK that requests, prayers, intercessions, and thanksgivings be offered for everyone, . . . that we may lead a quiet and peaceful life in all piety and dignity.

OCT.
18

—1 Tim 2:1-2

REFLECTION. Our heart can include in the decades of the Rosary all the events that comprise the life of the individual, the family, the nation, and all humankind.

It can include our own circumstances, those of our neighbor, and especially those of people dear to us. —*Pope John Paul II*

PRAYER. *O Mary, the Rosary beats out the rhythm of human life. Help me to meditate on the Mysteries of Jesus and apply them to life.*

 HAT does the Lord, your God, require of you but . . . that you love him, and serve the Lord, your God, with all your heart and all your soul?

OCT.
19

—Deut 10:12

REFLECTION. Cast yourself in spirit into the Heart of Mary.

Then love the Sovereign Good by means of this Heart that is so pure! —*St. Paul of the Cross*

PRAYER. *O Mary, your Immaculate Heart holds the secret of loving God. Teach me to love God with all my heart and to do His will in all things.*

B LESSED is the man who follows not the advice of the wicked . . . , but rejoices in the Law of the Lord and day and night meditates on his Law.

OCT. 20

—Ps 1:1-2

REFLECTION. Among the prayers that we profitably address to the Virgin Mother of God, the Rosary occupies a special place.

It is sometimes called the "Psalter of the Blessed Virgin" or the "Breviary of the Gospel and of the Christian life." — *Pope Pius XI*

PRAYER. *O Mary, your Rosary in its full form has fifteen decades and 150 Hail Marys, like the 150 Psalms. Grant me the same reverence for the Rosary that I have for the Psalms.*

A T that time, you were without Christ, excluded from the community of Israel, and strangers to the covenant, with no hope and without God in the world. — Eph 2:12

OCT. 21

REFLECTION. O Mary, I have no doubt that whenever we run to you, we shall obtain all that we desire.

Let those then who have no hope, hope in you. —*St. Bernard*

PRAYER. *O Mary, you are the Hope of the hopeless. Take pity on sinners and give them hope of conversion, so that you can then bring them back to your Divine Son.*

OR she herself goes about seeking those who are worthy of her, and she graciously appears to them as they tread life's paths, meeting them with all benevolence.

OCT. 22

—Wis 6:16

REFLECTION. The compassion and the love of this good Mother are great.

Indeed, they are so great that she does not even wait for our prayers but anticipates them.

—*St. Alphonsus Liguori*

PRAYER. *O Mary, you know my needs and my weaknesses. Come to my aid even when in my distraction I fail to call upon you.*

———————

EACE I bequeath to you; my peace I grant to you. Not as the world gives do I give to you. Do not let your hearts be fearful.

OCT. 23

—Jn 14:27

REFLECTION. Queen of Peace, it is through your Immaculate Heart that the God of peace has been given to the world.

Let this sweet peace reign in the Church and in our souls. —*St. John Eudes*

PRAYER. *O Mary, you are the Queen of Peace. Bring peace to my heart, so that I may work for peace in my family, in my Church, in my country, and in the world.*

ESUS went down with Mary and Joseph and came to Nazareth, and was subject to them; and his mother treasured all these things carefully in her heart. —Lk 2:51

OCT. 24

REFLECTION. In imitation of Jesus, Christians should love Mary and think the best of her.

They should take her as their Mother and love, serve, wait upon her, and like Jesus be completely obedient to her. —*St. Anthony Claret*

PRAYER. *O Mary, increase my love and regard for you as my Mother. Help me to serve you in all things, for in doing so I will be serving and obeying your Divine Son.*

 NOW the God of your father and serve him with wholehearted devotion and a willing soul, for the Lord searches every heart. —1 Chr 28:9

OCT. 25

REFLECTION. Imitate Mary, O faithful soul. Enter into the deep recesses of your heart, so that you may be purified spiritually and cleansed from your sins.

God places more value on goodwill in all we do than on the works themselves.

—*St. Lawrence Justinian*

PRAYER. *O Mary, you are the Model of purity of heart. Give me a right intention in all things, so that all my words and works may be pleasing to your Divine Son.*

Y dear children, for whom I am again in labor pains until Christ is formed in you! I wish I could be with you now. —Gal 4:19-20

REFLECTION. If Paul by his care and heartfelt tenderness gives birth to his children again and again till Christ be formed in them, how much more so does Mary!

In a manner far more holy and godlike, she begot her children by giving birth to the Word himself. *—Blessed Guerric of Igny*

PRAYER. *O Mary, you beget us in Christ. Help me to live as befits someone who has Christ as a Brother, God as a Father, and you as a Mother.*

E who provides for his father atones for sins; and he who respects his mother stores up riches. —Sir 3:3-4

REFLECTION. As the Mother of Christ, Mary is the Mother of our wisdom and justice, of our holiness and redemption.

She is more our Mother than the mother of our flesh. *—St. Aelred*

PRAYER. *O Mary, you are the Spiritual Mother of all Christians. Help me to be your devoted child by remaining true to my Church and to her teachings, which come from your Divine Son.*

HE fruit of the Spirit is charity, joy, peace, patience, kindness, goodness, faithfulness, modesty, and self-control. —Gal 5:22

OCT.
28

REFLECTION. When the Holy Spirit finds Mary in a soul, He flies to it.

He enters therein and communicates Himself to that soul in abundance.

—*St. Louis Grignion de Montfort*

PRAYER. *O Mary, you draw down upon souls the Holy Spirit with all His fruits. Grant that by being devoted to you I may receive these fruits without measure.*

S the heavens are exalted above the earth, so are my ways exalted above your ways and my thoughts higher than your thoughts. —Isa 55:9

OCT.
29

REFLECTION. If you can find the least instance of severity recorded about Mary in the Gospels, you may legitimately fear to approach her. But you will never find one.

So go to her cheerfully, and she will save you by her intercession. —*St. Bernard*

PRAYER. *O Mary, you are a most compassionate Mediatrix for all who come to you. Let me never fear to approach you.*

OW beautiful you are, how comely, my love, with your delights. —SS 7:7

OCT. 30

REFLECTION. Great was the love that Mary possessed.

So great indeed that it gave rise to that perfect beauty by which she captivated the Heart of her God! —*St. Thomas of Villanova*

PRAYER. *O Mary, you were filled with love for God and human beings. Help me to strive to share that love on earth so that I may share your glory in heaven.*

———

 OLD fast to [her], never let her go; guard her, for she is your life. —Prov 4:13

OCT. 31

REFLECTION. Has anyone ever come away from Mary troubled or saddened or ignorant of the heavenly Mysteries?

Who has not returned to everyday life gladdened and joyful because a request has been granted by the Mother of God?

—*St. Amadeus of Lausanne*

PRAYER. *O Mary, you are my life. Let me remain united to you all my days. Keep me from the path of sin and out of the clutches of the devil.*

DO not harm the earth or the sea or the trees until we have sealed the servants of our God on their foreheads. **NOV. 1**

—Rev 7:3

REFLECTION.   Those who possess great marks of predestination love, delight in, and recite the "Hail Mary."

And the more they belong to God, the more they love this prayer.

—*St. Louis Grignion de Montfort*

PRAYER.   *O Mary, all the Saints possessed the mark of devotion to the "Hail Mary." Grant that my devotion to you may increase and become for me a true pledge of my salvation.*

FATHER Abraham, have mercy on me. Send Lazarus to dip his finger in water and refresh my tongue, for I am tormented in these flames. **NOV. 2**

—Lk 16:24

REFLECTION.   Our Blessed Mother once said to me:

"I am the Mother of the Poor Souls. For my prayers serve to mitigate their sufferings every single hour that they remain in purgatory."

—*St. Bridget*

PRAYER.   *O Mary, you are the Mother of the Poor Souls in purgatory. Lessen their sufferings and grant them a speedy entrance into heavenly bliss.*

IS thought was holy and devout. Therefore, he had this expiatory sacrifice offered for the dead so that they might be delivered from their sin. — 2 Mac 12:45-46

NOV. 3

REFLECTION. The Blessed Virgin Mary has the power of delivering souls from purgatory by her prayers and by applying her merits for them.

This is especially true for souls that were devoted to her on earth. —*St. Bernardine of Siena*

PRAYER. *O Mary, you are Our Lady of Deliverance. Pray for us and for the Holy Souls in purgatory, especially those who were most devoted to you.*

VERY high priest chosen from among men is made their representative before God, to offer gifts and sacrifices to expiate sins. —Heb 5:1

NOV. 4

REFLECTION. O Holy Mother of God, pray for the priests your Son has chosen to serve the Church.

Help them by your intercession to be holy, zealous, and chaste. Enable them to become models of virtue in the service of the people of God. —*St. Charles Borromeo*

PRAYER. *O Mary, you are the Mother of Priests. Help me always to esteem the priests of the Church and to pray for them in their exalted work of sanctifying souls.*

O one who dwells there will say, "I am feeble." The people who dwell there shall have their sins forgiven.

NOV. 5

—Isa 33:24

REFLECTION. The Church calls Mary the "Queen of Mercy" because we believe she opens the abyss of God's mercy to whomever she wills, when she wills, and as she wills.

No sinner—no matter how great—who has Mary as protector is ever lost. —*St. Bernard*

PRAYER. *O Mary, obtain the conversion and pardon of hardened sinners. And grant me true sorrow for my sins and a firm purpose of amendment.*

———————

 UT he commanded the clouds above and the doors of heaven he opened . . . and gave them bread from heaven.

NOV. 6

— Ps 78:23-24

REFLECTION. We cannot enter a house without first speaking to the porter.

Similarly, we cannot enter heaven without calling upon the aid of the Blessed Virgin Mary who is the Portress of Heaven.

—*St. John Vianney*

PRAYER. *O Mary, you are the Portress of Heaven. Let me live every day in union with you, so that after my death you may open the doors of heaven to me for all eternity.*

DEATH has been swallowed up in victory. O death, where is your victory? . . . Where is your sting?

NOV.
7

—1 Cor 15:54-55

REFLECTION. Although we are sinners, let us be of good heart and feel certain that Mary will come to assist us at death.

We need only serve her with love for the remainder of our time in this world.

—St. Alphonsus Liguori

PRAYER. *O Mary, I give myself wholly to you. Watch over me in life and protect me especially in the hour of my death.*

———————

MARTHA, you are upset and troubled about many things; only one thing is necessary. Mary has chosen the better part and it will not be taken away from her.

NOV.
8

—Lk 10:41-42

REFLECTION. Our life on earth is filled with troubles and temptations.

We must let ourselves be captivated by Mary and model our life in some way upon her exemplary holiness.

—Pope Paul VI

PRAYER. *O Mary, you are our Model in Holiness. Teach me to follow you closely in life and so remain united with your Divine Son both on earth and in heaven.*

HE souls of the just are in the hand of God, and no torment can overtake them. . . . But they are at peace.

—Wis 3:1-3

REFLECTION. It is from Mary that we must look for the grace of a happy death.

This is very evident since the grace of final perseverance is the most important of all graces, inasmuch as it efficaciously consummates the work of everyone's salvation.

—*Pope Benedict XV*

PRAYER. *O Mary, you are the Mediatrix of All Grace. Grant me the graces I need during life and especially the grace of a happy death.*

 GIVE you a wise and understanding heart so that there will never have been anyone like you up to now, and after you there will never be one to equal you. —1 Ki 3:12

REFLECTION. Mary remains in the Church and is present in her in a maternal way.

She continues to reserve in her Heart all that the Church, the Mystical Body of her Son, lives and all that—in the Church—the human family lives as well as every person redeemed by Christ. —*Pope John Paul II*

PRAYER. *O Mary, you are the Mother of the Church. Reserve in your Heart the lives of all the faithful and watch over each one of us.*

E has come to the aid of Israel his servant, mindful of his mercy, according to his promise to our fathers, to Abraham and to his descendants forever. —Lk 1:54-55

REFLECTION. The Virgin Mother is constantly present on the journey of faith of the People of God toward the light.

This is shown in a special way by the Canticle of the Magnificat, which having welled up from the depth of Mary's faith at the Visitation ceaselessly reechoes in the heart of the Church down the centuries. —*Pope John Paul II*

PRAYER. *O Mary, your Magnificat is a favorite prayer for praising the gratuitousness of God's salvation for the poor and lowly. Help me to recite it daily.*

HE will come forth to meet the just man like a mother. . . . He will lean on her and not fall, rely on her and not be put to shame. —Sir 15:2-4

REFLECTION. Mary is the heart of the Church. From this heart there spring forth without interruption all the works of charity.

—*St. Anthony Claret*

PRAYER. *O Mary, increase my faith in the true Church of your Divine Son, and make that faith manifest itself every day in genuine works of charity.*

LESSED is the man who meditates on wisdom, . . . who reflects on her ways in his heart, and ponders her secrets.

—Sir 14:20-21

NOV.
13

REFLECTION.   Mary has a most tender love for all of us.

If she were to be praised all over the world, and if all human beings laid down their lives for her, it would be little compared with the honor we owe her.   —*St. Alphonsus Liguori*

PRAYER.   *O Mary, we owe you a debt of thanks and praise. Help me to show my gratitude by thanking you every day and by singing your praises to everyone I meet.*

OME, blessed of my Father, possess the kingdom prepared for you from the foundation of the world.

—Mt 25:34

NOV.
14

REFLECTION.   Mary, the Mother of our Lord, accompanied by the choirs of Angels, will come to meet you.

What a day of joy that will be for you!

—*St. Jerome*

PRAYER.   *O Mary, watch over me at every moment and keep me free from sin. Then upon my death, come to meet me and lead me to my eternal home in heaven.*

N times past, God spoke in partial and diverse ways to our fathers through the Prophets; in these last days, he spoke to us through his Son. —Heb 1:1-2

NOV. 15

REFLECTION. Mary is the Divine Page on which the Father wrote the Word of God, His Son. —*St. Albert the Great*

PRAYER. *O Mary, you reveal the Son of God to us. Let me contemplate you each day, so that I may get to know you better—and Jesus as well.*

———————

 EALTH and wages make life sweet, but better than either is finding a treasure. —Sir 40:18

NOV. 16

REFLECTION. Most holy Heart of Mary, the sole good I possess is the treasure you yourself have given me: the Sacred Heart of Jesus!

I offer Him to you now. Since He is infinite in value, I could do no more and you deserve no less. —*St. Gertrude*

PRAYER. *O Mary, let me appreciate the treasure we have in Jesus. Keep me close to Him all my life.*

FROM everyone to whom much has been given, much will be demanded; and from the one entrusted with more, more will be required. —Lk 12:48

REFLECTION. The Blessed Virgin once said to me: "You think that I obtained grace and virtues without effort.

"Know that I received no graces from God without great labor, constant prayer, ardent desires, and many tears and mortifications."
—*St. Elizabeth of Hungary*

PRAYER. *O Mary, you are the Model of Cooperation with Grace. Help me to cooperate fully with the graces you obtain for me.*

———————

THEY will praise me in the land of their exile as they invoke my name. —Bar 2:32

REFLECTION. Most holy Virgin Mary, your Name is so sweet and lovable that it cannot be uttered without inspiring love for you and God.

Those who love you need only to recall your Name to mind, and it is enough to console them and enkindle greater love. —*St. Bernard*

PRAYER. *O Mary, your Name is our consolation. Help me to have it ever on my lips and in my heart during my time on earth.*

OU . . . know me, you see me, you have tested my heart. —Jer 12:3

NOV.
19

REFLECTION. O Mary, you are the Virgin who captivates our hearts.

Introduce into heavenly joys the souls who venerate your Heart. —*St. John Eudes*

PRAYER. *O Mary, you are the Queen of Hearts. Take me under your care and help me to venerate your Heart temporally on earth and eternally in heaven.*

———————

HERE is immortality in kinship with [her], and pure delight in friendship with her, and inexhaustible wealth in the works of her hands. —Wis 8:17-18

NOV.
20

REFLECTION. Our good works pass through the hands of Mary and receive an increase in purity as well as in merit and intercessory value.

That is why they become much more capable of comforting the Holy Souls in purgatory.
—*St. Louis Grignion de Montfort*

PRAYER. *O Mary, purify my good works and apply them to the Holy Souls. Help especially those souls who were closest to me on earth.*

HEY who are planted in the house of the Lord will flourish in the courts of our God. —Ps 92:14

REFLECTION. The Blessed Virgin Mary was led to the Temple.

Thenceforward planted in the house of God, and cultivated by the Spirit, she like a fruitful olive tree became the abode of all virtues.

—*St. John Damascene*

PRAYER. *O Mary, in the Temple you grew in both body and soul. Let me always continue to grow in soul long after my body has stopped growing.*

—————————

 OUR word is a lamp for my feet and a light to my path. I have sworn . . . to keep your just decrees. —Ps 119:105-106

REFLECTION. To believe means to abandon oneself to the truth of the word of the living God.

Mary, who by the eternal will of the Most High stands at the very center of the "inscrutable ways" and "unsearchable judgments" of God, conforms herself to them in the dim light of faith, accepting fully everything that is decreed in the Divine plan. —*Pope John Paul II*

PRAYER. *O Mary, you heeded God's Word above all others. Help me to listen to that Word and keep it every day of my life no matter*

OT only are you beautiful to behold, but you are eloquent in your wisdom. If you do as you have promised, your God shall be my God. —Jud 11:23

NOV.
23

REFLECTION. Mary found glory for herself and for others, because through her the gate of heaven was opened to us.

For inasmuch as God came down to us through her, it is right that through her we should ascend to God. —*St. Bonaventure*

PRAYER. *O Mary, you bring God to us and us to God. Help me to follow your inspirations every day, so that I may remain united with your Divine Son throughout my life.*

 HATEVER is true, whatever is noble, whatever is just, whatever is pure, whatever is lovable, whatever is admirable . . . think about these things. —Phil 4:8

NOV.
24

REFLECTION. God has deposited in Mary the fullness of all that is good.

So if we have any hope, any grace, any salvation, we should realize that it all comes to us through Mary. —*St. Bernard*

PRAYER. *O Mary, all spiritual goods come to us from God through you. Teach me to ask only for those things that help my spiritual growth.*

THE spirit is what gives life; the flesh counts for nothing. The words that I have spoken . . . are spirit and life.

NOV. 25

—Jn 6:63

REFLECTION. The Mother and Mistress of Wisdom speaks few words, but each is filled with great depth of meaning.

We read that the Mother of Christ spoke seven times, seven words filled with wisdom!

—*St. Bernardine*

PRAYER. *O Mary, your words like those of Jesus are spirit and life. Help me to meditate on them every day, for—even though they are few—they are filled with meaning for me.*

ANYTHING that you ask for . . . I will grant, so that the Father may be glorified in the Son.

NOV. 26

—Jn 14:13

REFLECTION. O most dear Mary, blessed is the person who loves you!

If I love Mary, I am certain of perseverance, and I will obtain from God whatever I want.

—*St. John Berchmans*

PRAYER. *O Mary, you have great power with God. Obtain my legitimate requests from your Divine Son and ensure my perseverance in grace until my death.*

171

FOR the joy that was set before him he endured the cross, despising the shame, and is seated at the right hand of the throne of God. —Heb 12:2

NOV. 27

REFLECTION. Mary imparts to her children both their crosses and the grace to carry them patiently and even cheerfully.

Thus it is that the crosses she lays upon those who belong to her are steeped in sweetness rather than filled with bitterness.

—*St. Louis Grignion de Montfort*

PRAYER. *O Mary, I am often overwhelmed by the crosses God sends me. Help me to bear them patiently and without complaining.*

GOD'S firm foundation stands unshaken, bearing this seal: "The Lord knows who belong to him." —2 Tim 2:19

NOV. 28

REFLECTION. If we are true servants of Mary and obtain her protection, we will most certainly be enrolled in the Book of Life.

Whoever bears the mark of devotion to Mary, God recognizes as His own.

—*St. Alphonsus Liguori*

PRAYER. *O Mary, let me never waver in my true devotion to you. May it impart spiritual happiness during my life and ensure eternal happiness at my death.*

O me, the very least of all saints, this grace has been given, to announce to the Gentiles the good news of the unfathomable riches of Christ.
—Eph 3:8

REFLECTION. The more her children entrust themselves to Mary, the nearer she leads them to the "unfathomable riches of Christ."

And to the same degree they recognize more and more clearly the dignity and the vocation of human beings.
—*Pope John Paul II*

PRAYER. *O Mary, help me to grow in the knowledge and love of your Divine Son Jesus each day and to see Him in all things.*

ITHOUT faith it is not possible to please God. For anyone who comes to him must have faith that God exists and that he rewards those who try to find him.
—Heb 11:6

REFLECTION. Mary is not only the sublime "type" of the creature redeemed by the merits of Christ but also the "type" of humankind on the pilgrimage of faith.

Her faith leads us in the reality of the Gospel!
—*Pope Paul VI*

PRAYER. *O Mary, you are our Model in the pilgrimage of faith. Grant that I may imitate your faith as I make my way along the bewildering paths of this world.*

O not let your hearts be downcast. **DEC.** You believe in God; believe also in me. —Jn 14:1 **1**

REFLECTION. O happy confidence! O perfect refuge! The Mother of God is my Mother.

What firm trust we should have, then, since our salvation depends on the judgment of a good Brother and a tender Mother! —*St. Anselm*

PRAYER. *O Mary, you are the Mother of Salvation. Let me place all my trust in you and in your Divine Son—no matter what dangers I may encounter during life.*

 WILL give them a new heart and put a **DEC.** new spirit within them; I will remove the heart of stone from their flesh. **2** —Ezek 11:19

REFLECTION. Give your heart completely to Mary.

And beg her to make it like the Heart of her Divine Son. —*St. John Eudes*

PRAYER. *O Mary, I willingly give you my heart to be conformed to the Heart of Jesus. Grant me the grace to possess the sentiments of your Divine Son.*

FOR I will make you renowned and praised among all the peoples of the world . . . says the Lord.

DEC.

3

—Zep 3:20

REFLECTION. At times, I have failed to place an image of our Savior's Mother beside His Cross.

At such times, I have always found the peoples rebellious to the Gospel! —*St. Francis Xavier*

PRAYER. *O Mary, you are the Mother of the Missions. Enable me to help spread the Gospel—abroad by prayer and at home by the witness of a Christian life.*

SINCE we belong to the day, we must be composed. Let us put on the breastplate of faith and charity and the helmet that is the hope of salvation.

DEC.

4

—1 Thes 5:8

REFLECTION. As long as I keep alive my hope in you, O Mother of God, I shall be safe.

I will fight and overcome enemies with this one shield—your protection and your powerful help. —*St. John Damascene*

PRAYER. *O Mary, you are the Queen of spiritual victories. Grant me the strength to overcome all the assaults of the devil during life and especially at the hour of death.*

E took the bread, . . . and gave it to them, saying, "This is my body, which is being given for you; do this in remembrance of me." —Lk 22:19

DEC. 5

REFLECTION. Mary's Motherhood is particularly noted and experienced by the Christian people at the Sacred Banquet at which Christ, His "true body born of the Virgin Mary," becomes present.

Mary guides the faithful to the Eucharist.

—*Pope John Paul II*

PRAYER. *O Mary, you are Our Lady of the Eucharist. Help me to know, love, and live the Mass by striving to participate fully, actively, and consciously in every Mass I attend.*

LESSED are you, and deserving of all praise . . . and glorious is your name forever.

—Dan 3:26

DEC. 6

REFLECTION. The Name of Mary contains in itself the brilliance of the virtues, the sweet reflection of modesty, and the sacrifice agreeable to God.

It is the sign of hospitality and the center of sanctity. —*St. Peter Chrysologus*

PRAYER. *O Mary, your holy Name is glorious forever. Grant me the grace to revere it, call upon it every day, and teach it to others—especially my relatives, friends, and benefactors.*

THOSE he foreknew he also predestined to be changed into the likeness of his Son. And those he predestined he also . . . made righteous.

DEC. 7

—Rom 8:29-30

REFLECTION. Think often of the Blessed Virgin with love.

Those who have received the grace to do so possess a great sign of predestination.

—*St. Ambrose*

PRAYER. *O Mary, let me meditate often on you and on your Divine Son. Teach me to be like Him and thus strive to attain the holiness God has decreed for me.*

 ALL of us at one time lived among them in the cravings of our flesh . . . and we were by nature children of wrath, like the others.

DEC. 8

—Eph 2:3

REFLECTION. How far from this woe of those who are born "children of wrath" was the most holy Nativity of Mary!

She was free not only from original sin but also from the fuel of misery, insofar as it leads to sin, for she was conceived without stain.

—*St. Bonaventure*

PRAYER. *O Mary, conceived without sin, pray for us who have recourse to you.*

THE angel said to her, "Do not be afraid, Mary, for you have found grace with God." —Lk 1:30

DEC. 9

REFLECTION. The Immaculate Conception is the name that reveals with precision who Mary is.

Mary is profoundly holy in the totality of her existence, from her very beginnings.

—*Pope John Paul II*

PRAYER. *O Mary, you are all-holy. Help me to strive after holiness by doing the will of God as it becomes clear to me through each day's events.*

RISE up and shine! Your light has come and the glory of the Lord has risen upon you. —Isa 60:1

DEC. 10

REFLECTION. The Holy Spirit did not describe Mary in the Gospels but left it to you to picture her in your heart.

In this way, you might comprehend that there is no grace, no perfection, and no glory conceivable in a simple creature that is lacking to her. —*St. Thomas of Villanova*

PRAYER. *O Mary, help me to meditate often on your life in the Mysteries of Christ. May I come to appreciate the true glory that is yours.*

ITHIN her is a spirit that is intelligent, holy, unique, manifold, subtle, mobile, clear, undefiled.

—Wis 7:22

DEC. 11

REFLECTION. How good Mary is! How beautiful she is!

How worthy she is of all respect!

—*St. John Eudes*

PRAYER. *O Mary, you are all-beautiful, and there is no stain of sin in you. Grant that I may praise you as you deserve—both by my words and by my actions.*

———————

OU have visited the earth and watered it; you have enriched it abundantly.

—Ps 65:10

DEC. 12

REFLECTION. Mary is the fruitful Virgin everywhere.

Thus, she produces in the soul wherein she dwells purity of heart and of body, purity of intention and of purpose, and fruitfulness in good works. —*St. Louis Grignion de Montfort*

PRAYER. *O Mary, today the Church recalls your appearance as Our Lady of Guadalupe. As I honor you under this glorious title, grant me the graces I need for my state of life.*

179

OW sweet are your words to my taste, sweeter than honey to my mouth! —Ps 119:103

 DEC.
13

REFLECTION. The seven words (or phrases) of Mary found in the Gospels are voiced in accord with a wonderful progression and order.

They impart to the devout soul the ardor of a holy love. —*St. Bernardine of Siena*

PRAYER. *O Mary, help me to emulate what each of your words imparts: virginal reserve (Lk 1:34); zealous service (Lk 1:38a); faithful obedience (Lk 1:38b); joyful praise (Lk 1:46-55); authoritative gentleness (Lk 2:48); tender charity (Jn 2:3); and firm faith (Jn 2:5).*

OD said, "Honor your father and your mother," and "Whoever abuses father or mother shall be put to death." —Mt 15:4

DEC.
14

REFLECTION. Jesus said: "Honor your father and your mother."

Therefore, in order that He might observe His own decree, He gave all grace and honor to His Mother! —*St. Methodius*

PRAYER. *O Mary, as the Mother of the Lord of All, you received all grace and honor. Help me to join my voice to that of all the Angels and Saints in praising you.*

ET us live in peace with God through our Lord Jesus Christ, by whom we have been introduced through faith to God's grace that we now enjoy.

DEC.
15

—Rom 5:2

REFLECTION.   Mary, you have found grace because you desired and sought it.

You have found Uncreated Grace—that is, God Himself became your Son—and with that grace you have found and obtained every uncreated good. —*St. Albert the Great*

PRAYER.   *O Mary, you are the Mother of Uncreated Grace. Grant that I may seek your Divine Son in everything I do and say.*

E are fools for Christ. . . . When reviled, we bless; when persecuted, we bear it; when maligned, we respond with kindness.

DEC.
16

—1 Cor 4:10-13

REFLECTION.   Those who burn with the fire of Divine Love are children of the Immaculate Heart of Mary, and wherever they go they enkindle that flame.

Nothing distresses them; they rejoice in poverty, labor strenuously, welcome hardships, laugh off false accusations, and rejoice in anguish. —*St. Anthony Claret*

PRAYER.   *O Mary, teach me to offer all my prayers, works, and sufferings of each day in union with your Immaculate Heart to Jesus for the salvation of the world.*

181

PRAISE the Lord in his holy place. . . . Praise him for his marvelous works; praise him for his lofty majesty.

DEC.
17

—Ps 150:1-2

REFLECTION. Praise God for the great blessings He bestowed on Mary and for choosing her to be His Mother.

Such a prayer of praise will be most pleasing to the Blessed Virgin. —*St. Jane Frances de Chantal*

PRAYER. *O Mary, let me praise and thank God for the mighty deeds He has done in and through you. Let me thank Him especially for the graces I have received through you.*

―――――――

THE Lord, your God, is with you— your Savior. He will exult over you with gladness and renew you with his love.

DEC.
18

—Zep 3:17

REFLECTION. What greater prodigy could the world behold than a woman become the Mother of God and a God clothed in human flesh?

Mary, by her humility, became the Mother of her Creator. The Creator, in His goodness, became the Son of His own creature!

—*St. Alphonsus Liguori*

PRAYER. *O Mary, you took an active part in the greatest event the world has known. Grant that I may be ever open to God's call and eager to serve Him.*

GIVE thanks to my God every time I remember you, and I pray always with joy for all of you. —Phil 1:3

DEC. 19

REFLECTION. Through Mary, the miserable obtain mercy, the graceless find grace, and sinners receive pardon.

The weak gain strength, earthlings acquire heavenly things, mortals win life, and pilgrims find their country! —*St. Augustine*

PRAYER. *O Mary, you are forever interceding for us before God's throne. Help me to come to you in every need—whether it be of soul or of body.*

 Y the grace of God I have become what I am, and his grace in me has not been fruitless. —1 Cor 15:10

DEC. 20

REFLECTION. May the glorious Virgin bestow on you all the graces whose source is her Heart! —*St. Bonaventure*

PRAYER. *O Mary, you are the Mediatrix of All Graces. Pour forth in my heart all the graces that were in your Heart and made you pleasing to the God of all.*

HE shall be great and shall be called the Son of the Most High . . . and he shall reign over the house of Jacob forever, and of his kingdom there shall be no end. —Lk 1:32-33

DEC.
21

REFLECTION. The Fathers of the Church recognized the tremendous praise heaped on Mary in the Scriptures.

She is singled out as having a King for her father (the noble David) and the King of kings and Lord of lords for her Son, Whose reign will never end. —*St. Peter Canisius*

PRAYER. *O Mary, you are Queen of all because your Son is the King of kings. Grant that I may offer you every day the praise and honor you deserve.*

BEHOLD, I stand knocking at the door. If anyone listens to my voice and opens the door, I will be his guest and eat with him. —Rev 3:20

DEC.
22

REFLECTION. Open your heart to faith, O Blessed Virgin, your lips to praise, your womb to the Creator.

See, the Desired of All Nations is at your door, knocking to enter. Arise in faith, hasten in devotion, open in praise and thanksgiving.

—*St. Bernard*

PRAYER. *O Mary, you are the Model of Openness. Teach me to open my heart to you and to your Divine Son, so that you can dwell within it forever.*

HAVE come as a light into the world, so that everyone who believes in me may not have to stay in darkness. —Jn 12:46

DEC. 23

REFLECTION. The Mother of God, the most pure Virgin, carried the True Light in her arms and brought Him to those who lay in darkness.

We too should carry a light for all to see and reflect the radiance of the True Light as we hasten to meet Him. —*St. Sophronius*

PRAYER. *O Mary, you are the Mother of the True Light Who enlightens the world. Help me to bear witness to that Light all the days of my life.*

HILE they were there, the time came for the child to be born, and [Mary] brought forth her firstborn son. —Lk 2:6-7

DEC. 24

REFLECTION. O Mary, if the Holy One born of your womb is really incarnate, then you, must truly be called the Mother of God.

For you have, in absolute truth, brought forth God! —*St. Sophronius*

PRAYER. *O Mary, you are the Mother of God for you brought forth the Son of God. Teach me how to bring forth Jesus in the lives of all those I will encounter this day.*

AND the Word became flesh and dwelt among us. And we saw his glory, the glory as of the only-begotten of the Father, full of grace and truth. —Jn 1:14

DEC.
25

REFLECTION. Today Mary is a heaven for us, because she bears God within herself.

The Most High God has abased Himself and made His dwelling in her, so that He might bring about our salvation. —*St. Ephrem*

PRAYER. *O Mary, the Son of God became man in you, so that He might become like us and save us. Help me to remain ever united with you, so that I may become like Jesus.*

THE hour is coming . . . when true worshipers will worship the Father in Spirit and truth. For the Father wants such worshipers. —Jn 4:23

DEC.
26

REFLECTION. True devotion to the Blessed Virgin is internal, starting from the spirit and the heart.

It flows from the esteem we bear toward Mary, the sublime idea we have of her greatness, and the love we feel for her.

—*St. Louis Grignion de Montfort*

PRAYER. *O Mary, let my devotion toward you be always much more than external. Let it flow naturally from heartfelt love and esteem for you.*

INDEED, I have calmed and set at rest my soul like a child on its mother's lap, . . . thus is my soul within me. —Ps 131:2

DEC. 27

REFLECTION. True devotion to the Blessed Virgin is tender. It is full of confidence in Mary, like a child's confidence in its mother.

This ensures that we will run to Mary in all our needs. —*St. Louis Grignion de Montfort*

PRAYER. *O Mary, let my devotion toward you lead me to you in all my sorrows and needs with simplicity, trust, and tenderness.*

 STRIVE diligently to support your faith with virtue, virtue with knowledge, knowledge with self-control, self-control with perseverance, perseverance with piety, piety with mutual love, mutual love with charity. —2 Pet 1:5-7

DEC. 28

REFLECTION. True devotion to the Blessed Virgin is *holy*. It leads us to avoid sin and imitate the virtues of Mary: her deep humility, lively faith, ready obedience, continuous prayer, universal mortification, Divine purity, ardent charity, heroic patience, angelic sweetness, and heavenly wisdom.

—*St. Louis Grignion de Montfort*

PRAYER. *O Mary, let my devotion toward you lead me to avoid sin and imitate the virtues enumerated above, which are the ten principal virtues you practiced on earth.*

I N this world you will have affliction, but take heart, I have overcome the world.

—Jn 16:33

DEC. 29

REFLECTION. True devotion to the Blessed Virgin is *constant*. It strengthens us in good and makes us courageous in opposing the world, the flesh, and the devil.

Those devoted to Mary live by the faith of Jesus and Mary, not the sentiments of nature.

—*St. Louis Grignion de Montfort*

PRAYER. *O Mary, let my devotion toward you give me daily courage in the face of temptations from the world, the flesh, and the devil.*

D O not be anxious about your life, what you will eat, . . . or about your body, what you will put on. . . . Will not God . . . do much more for you?

—Mt 6:25-

DEC. 30

REFLECTION. True devotion to the Blessed Virgin is *disinterested*. It inspires us to seek not ourselves but God alone in His holy Mother.

True clients of Mary serve her not because they seek earthly gain, nor even corporal or spiritual well-being, but because she deserves to be served—and God alone in her!

—*St. Louis Grignion de Montfort*

PRAYER. *O Mary, let my devotion toward you give me a tranquil attitude about life and lead me to serve you and your Divine Son diligently all my days.*

AY to the fainthearted: Take courage, fear not! Behold your God— . . . he will come to save you.

DEC.
31

—Isa 35:4

REFLECTION. If the horror of sin terrifies you and the voice of conscience overwhelms you, if the fear of judgment, the depths of sadness, and the abyss of despair assail you, think of Mary!

In dangers, troubles, and sins, think of Mary and call upon her! —*St. Bernard*

PRAYER. *O Mary, at year's end, the weight of my sins frightens me. Intercede for me with your Divine Son Jesus, so that I may attain the salvation He won for me!*

PRAYER TO MARY

Composed by Pope John Paul II for the Marian Year

MOTHER of the Redeemer,
[in this year dedicated to you,]
with great joy we call you blessed.

In order to carry out His providential plan of
    salvation,
God the Father chose you before the creation of
    the world.
You believed in His love and obeyed His word.

The Son of God desired you for His Mother
when He became man to save the human race.
You received Him with ready obedience and
    undivided heart.

The Holy Spirit loved you as His mystical
    spouse
and He filled you with singular gifts.
You allowed yourself to be led
by His hidden and powerful action.

On the eve of the third Christian Millennium,
we entrust to you the Church
which acknowledges you and invokes you as
    Mother.
On earth you preceded the Church in the pil-
    grimage of faith:
comfort her in her difficulties and trials,

and make her always the sign and instrument
of intimate union with God
and of the unity of the whole human race.

To you, Mother of Christians,
we entrust in a special way
the peoples who are celebrating
[during the Marian Year]
the sixth Centenary or the Millennium
of their acceptance of the Gospel.
Their long history is profoundly marked by de-
    votion to you.
Turn toward them your loving glance;
give strength to those who are suffering for the
    faith.

To you, Mother of the human family and of the
    nations,
we confidently entrust the whole of humanity,
with its hopes and fears.
Do not let it lack the light of true wisdom.
Guide its steps in the ways of peace.
Enable all to meet Christ,
the Way and the Truth and the Life.

Sustain us, O Virgin Mary, on our journey of
    faith
and obtain for us the grace of eternal salva-
    tion.
O clement, O loving, O sweet Mother of God
and our Mother, Mary!

OTHER OUTSTANDING CATHOLIC BOOKS

DICTIONARY OF MARY—New and invaluable book that clearly sets forth the place of Mary in the Church and in the life of Catholics, her titles, authenticated apparitions, shrines, as well as Marian prayers and many other topics. **Ask for No. 367**

DAILY REFLECTIONS WITH MARY—By Rev. Rawley Myers. A beautifully illustrated and printed book that gives thirty-one prayerful Marian reflections plus a large selection of prayers to Our Lady. Every page is written out of deep love for Mary and inculcates a great devotion to her. **Ask for No. 372**

PRAYERS TO MARY—By Most Rev. Virgilio Noè. A beautiful book that gives prayers to Mary from various liturgies of the Church and Christians throughout the centuries as well as the more well-known prayers to Our Lady. Illustrated in color. **Ask for No. 210**

TREASURY OF NOVENAS—By Rev. Lawrence Lovasik, S.V.D. More than forty popular Novenas carefully arranged for private prayer in accord with the Liturgical Year on the Feasts of Jesus, Mary, and Favorite Saints. Illustrated in color. **Ask for No. 345**

THE GLORIES OF MARY—By St. Alphonsus. Adapted and very readable modern version of a classic book about the Blessed Virgin. Large type, illustrated. **Ask for No. 360**

MARY MY HOPE—By Rev. L. Lovasik, S.V.D. Popular book of devotions to Mary. New Vatican II edition. Large type, illustrated. **No. 365**

IMITATION OF MARY—By Rev. A. de Rouville, S.J. Companion volume to the **Imitation of Christ.** Large type, illustrated. **Ask for No. 330**

THE MYSTERY OF THE ROSARY—By Rev. Marc Tremeau, O.P. Completely new and up-to-date explanation of the Rosary. This book will help deepen the prayer life of all who read it. **Ask for No. 105**

PRAY THE ROSARY—By Rev. J. M. Lelen. The most popular, handy, purse-size Rosary booklet. Each Mystery is gloriously illustrated in full color with appropriate text. **Ask for No. 40**

WHEREVER CATHOLIC BOOKS ARE SOLD